Letters for
BRIAN
*Writing through the silence
of dementia*

Karen R Johnson

Copyright © 2025 (Karen Johnson)

All rights reserved worldwide.

No part of this book may be reproduced by any mechanical, photographic, or electronic processes, or in the form of a phonographic recording. Nor may it be stored in a retrieval system, transmitted or otherwise be copied for any public or private use other than for 'fair use' - as brief quotations embodied in articles and reviews, without prior written permission of the author.

ISBN: (pbk) 978-0-6459237-7-3
        (eBook) 978-0-6459237-8-0

A catalogue record for this book is available from the National Library of Australia

Author: Karen Johnson

Title: *Letters for Brian*

Genre: Memoir

Published by Write Angles Press

Edited by Emma Driver

Typesetting and cover design by Claire McGregor

Front cover image: Brian aged about 22 years in 1978, wearing a rep T-shirt for the "Country" Rugby League Team. The epitome of health and fitness.

For my husband, whose voice I will always hear. He gave me more strength, love and support than I could ever repay. And for my supporters who held me up – during and after.

Contents

Foreword: Roy Masters 1
Preface 5
Prologue: July 2010 9
1   Inseparable: Dapto High School, 1973 11
2   A family across the world 17
3   Road to diagnosis 25
4   Life goes on 33
5   Home and away 43
6   Adjustments 53
7   The complications of intimacy 57
8   Teamwork 61
9   Friends who give 65
10 On the road 69
11 A man of words 73
12 How not to help 77
13 Shared history 81
14 A less social life 85
15 The Happiness Project, part 1 91
16 How to care 95
17 A sensational service 105
18 The bloody awful week 109
19 Band of brothers 121
20 Respite? Not quite 125
21 Aftershocks 133

22	The Happiness Project, part 2	137
23	Joyce	141
24	On the home front	143
25	Is everyone still there?	147
26	The toughest decision	151
27	Experts by our side	157
28	Welcome visitors	159
29	Quiet house	163
30	Care and dedication	165
31	After life	167
32	A shrinking world	171
33	Stay with me	175
34	Our final days	179
35	How to say goodbye	187
36	The send-off	193
37	To Garry	201
38	You are not with me	205
	Epilogue: November 2024	207
	From Brian: A true story from Brian's childhood	215

Foreword

Roy Masters

Johnno was the antithesis of the rugby league players of his era. He was a near teetotaller at a time it was mandatory to go to the pub after training. He was blond-haired and handsome in a league of facial scars and missing teeth. He was a highly educated dux of his school while many of his opponents were labourers or truck drivers. He was deeply moral while others strayed. He was uncomfortable with the physical nature of rugby league, while some of his teammates relished it. He was a devoted family man in a code which tested relationships. Yet he was immensely popular and respected.

His teammate at Warrington, Les Boyd, aka 'the baby faced assassin', was the reverse of Brian. Whereas Les became fired up after face-slapping sessions when we were both at Wests, Brian's first words to me when I joined the Dragons were, 'Please, no face slapping.' Yet Les and Brian became great mates, with Les being the godfather to both of Brian's children. As Les says, 'You couldn't meet a nicer person. He was a very smart footballer and good to be around. He was very ethical, very witty. One of the best blokes I met playing football.'

Life dealt Brian and Karen a cruel blow when he succumbed to early onset dementia. Looking back, the signs were there when I coached him at the Dragons. His teammates nicknamed him 'Better Brakes' because, as a fullback, he sometimes slowed up as he approached the defensive line. He reasoned that it was counterproductive to be rendered semi-concussed in a tackle, since it lessened his effectiveness later in the game. I argued that he had to make the opposition earn their tackles. But perhaps he was already sensitive to head knocks. Many of my ex-players phone me in fear of their possible coming dementia but many are eight-schooners-of-beer-a-day men. If dementia is associated with AGE – where A stands for age, G for genetics and E for environment – Brian died at 59, ate healthily, was a fitness fanatic who led everyone on the 400-metre circuits of Kogarah Oval and drank alcohol only on Christmas Day.

If Brian had been born perhaps only five years earlier, he could have been the poster boy for the 1989 Tina Turner campaign when the New South Wales Rugby League were promoting handsome, educated players to win over the female demographic. After all, Brian read PE textbooks while others only skimmed the sports pages of the tabloids. Once, when an over-zealous trainer ran the Dragons into the ground at the Tuesday-night training session after a loss, he went home to his PE textbooks and underlined the relevant pages demonstrating how punishing players can be counterproductive.

He then printed them off and handed them to me at the next training session.

He was selfless. When I replaced him as fullback for Glenn Burgess in 1985, he volunteered, 'Burgo is playing better than me.' And on the day of that year's grand final, when he played in the successful reserve-grade premiership team, he said, 'I want you guys to win more than anything.'

When the position as inaugural head coach of the rugby league program at the Australian Institute of Sport came up and Brian was an applicant, I was on the board of the Australian Sports

Commission and in a position to help him.

The AIS program initially catered for young lads from Indigenous families and those from remote rural areas – young fellows whose talents needed to be nurtured before being recruited to Sydney clubs – a perfect role for Johnno.

The other shortlisted candidate was Mal Meninga, who had just finished his fabulous career with the Raiders.

But Brian, with his background as a teacher, was preferred and, as it transpired, Mal's star took on another more spectacular trajectory.

When we last met, I noted his speech faltering, with his AIS assistants subtly and loyally finishing his sentences.

Years before, Brian had read a travel piece I wrote in *The Sydney Morning Herald* on a visit to Oradour-sur-Glane, the French village where a German tank battalion slaughtered 642 villagers, including 247 women and 205 children for reasons still mysterious.

He took his young AIS team to the village every year until 2011.

The village remains today as it was in June 1944, abandoned, with rusted bikes and burnt-out cars, a reminder of man's inhumanity to man.

The words 'humanitarian' and 'rugby league' rarely appear in the same sentence but Brian, particularly as father, friend, husband and AIS coach, united them.

For most of the book, Karen details her confrontation with Brian's dementia and it is written in simple, yet beautiful language. It takes us on a journey from her being 'the world's most dedicated girlfriend' to a devoted carer of a man we loved and respected. While Karen's story offers advice to partners of those suffering dementia, it deserves a wider readership because, essentially, it is a love story.

Preface

My husband and I had the best life. Totally complete. The best marriage. Two beautiful sons. A happy family. A household that ran on quiet routines with no real hiccups. Decent jobs. A great income. Wonderful friends.

We never made great plans or set unrealistic goals. We were just happy. When something took our fancy, we bought it, or we booked to go there. We were spontaneous.

We were easily pleased, really. No designer labels or fancy cars. Simple things enjoyed together.

Easy. Until it wasn't.

My wonderful husband, Brian Johnson, was diagnosed with younger onset dementia.

Then he died. Too young. Too soon. Too horribly.

In the past few years, I have acquired a better understanding of chronic traumatic encephalopathy, or CTE – 'footballers' dementia'. I want others to understand what it is too. It frightens me to think that parents who want their children to play contact sports dismiss the risks associated with concussion and memory loss. 'If they can't remember things when they're old, so what?' I hear them say. 'It happens to all of us anyway.'

So this memoir has a purpose. I want to help and to educate others, and to assist anyone who is struggling with dementia – as the carer or the cared for. There are many more dementias than CTE, and all of them are distressing, no matter what symptoms they cause.

I want to track my memories of my life with Brian, to document the parts of Brian's life that are not rugby league statistics on Wikipedia.

I also hope it will help my children understand me.

I want people to have a better understanding of what dementia – in any of its forms – looks like, and what it means to care for someone with dementia. With the support of family, friends and professional organisations, caring is easier than you think it will be – and at times harder than anything you could ever imagine.

Dementia can be considered a bit of a joke at times by those not yet touched by it. 'Old timers' disease', some people still call it. They think 'memory problems' mean that you cannot recall someone's name, or where you parked the car.

But memory is what we rely on for everything we do, every day. And no one ever thinks memory loss can happen to anyone so young.

Think of all the things that we instinctively know how to do. How to hold a knife and fork. How to cut our food and get it to our mouths. If we walk to the bathroom to clean our teeth, we pick up our toothbrush. We learn these skills as children, and as adults they feel innate.

Think back to when you could not tie your shoes. I still remember how painstakingly I practised, with my mum helping me, before I started school. When my first day at kindergarten rolled around, I proudly walked into class with laces I had tied all by myself, and before long I could tie them without thinking about it. 'Muscle memory' is not really the muscle remembering. It is a pathway we create in our brains from practice. We do not think about our everyday tasks. We just do them – because we remember how to do them.

As Brian's brain became more and more affected, I watched his most basic memories erode. Every little thing he could do independently for his whole life suddenly required my instruction and assistance. I once watched Brian go to clean his teeth, pick up a disposable razor and put toothpaste on it. He had some memory of what his purpose in the bathroom was, but he had forgotten which tool on the sink did what. Luckily, I was with him and stopped him before he had a chance to put the razor in his mouth.

Another time, I'd heard him talking and laughing in the bathroom. When I asked what he was doing, he explained that the bloke in there was making him laugh by pulling faces at him, and he was pulling faces back at that bloke. 'That bloke' was his own reflection; he had forgotten what a mirror was and how it worked. Fortunately, that bloke was very friendly and funny. He could have been angry and scary – and that may have led to broken mirrors, blood and distress.

So, no – whatever else it is, dementia isn't a joke.

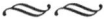

In this book are many letters I wrote during the last years of Brian's life. Almost none of them were sent. They were just for me.

Some were written in frustration and anger to those I felt had let us down. Some were to thank people who held us up and helped get us through the last horrible years of Brian's illness. But I wrote most of them to Brian, to tell him the things I wanted to explain. They were my way of debriefing after what were often long and tiring days, and my way of communicating with the man I had been able to discuss everything with for almost 40 years.

My letters are not comprehensive. There were people in our lives who I did not write to. I wrote when I needed to analyse something. When I was not too tired. Sometimes the comfort I got from the people around me calmed me and I had no reason to write. I did not keep a comprehensive diary.

But I am glad I wrote the letters. They are valuable to me now as I have forgotten just how hard the little day-to-day things were for Brian, and for me. I want to remember and share our experiences, so others may know what to expect.

These chapters don't run in strict chronological order. It is our story, but it is not a novel with a neat plot. I just want to indicate what it felt like for him go through such a long decline to the end of his life, and how it felt to care for him.

I do not want to take away any of Brian's dignity.

I do not want anyone held personally responsible for mistakes made in his care. I made plenty of mistakes too.

I *do* want professionals to understand how important care is, in every detail, and how cutting costs and corners has devastating impacts on people.

I want people to make informed decisions about contact sports for their children.

I want to thank some people – publicly and loudly – for the little things and for the big things they gave to Brian and to me: their time, their kindness, their friendship. For some of them, it was their job, and they did it well. For others, it was from their love for him. It is hard to adequately repay love that is given so selflessly.

I hope this book achieves some of those things.

I write with grief. After nine years, I am able to put my grief aside a little, in a place where it does not hurt as much anymore, but there will always be a hole in my heart left by Brian.

I do not want that hole to heal. I always want to miss him.

Prologue

July 2010

I had just checked into a hotel in Bruges, Belgium, when my telephone rang. It was Brian.

'Please don't hang up on me this time,' he said, loudly and quickly, obviously distraught. I could hear he was crying. 'I promise I have not had any women in our house. I would never do that to you.'

I did not know what he was talking about. It was the first time we had spoken in two days. I had never – I would *never* – hang up on him.

I assured him that I trusted him. That I had not hung up on him. That it had never even crossed my mind that he would have a woman in our house while I was away.

Confused, I told him I loved him and that I honestly did not know what he was talking about. It took some time, but he eventually calmed down and we talked about the possibility of someone playing a prank on him. Although that seemed very unlikely, I was angry that one of his friends could have called him and tricked him in that way.

Brian had seemed a little unwell before I'd left Australia, but the visit to France was a journey I had to take. My 72-year-old mother had been invited to an Australian Government ceremony in France for the lost soldiers of the Battle of Fromelles in July 1916. One of those lost soldiers was my great-uncle, Benedict Dunstan. He had been injured in the battle at Pheasant Wood, captured by the Germans and died a day later, on 20 July 1916, aged just 23. My mum's DNA had been used to help identify his body.

20 July is my birthday. Because of that anniversary, I had always felt like Uncle Ben was my special uncle, my soldier.

If I hadn't joined Mum for the trip, she would not have been able to attend the ceremony – or the luncheon to which she had been invited, which included King Charles, at the time the Prince of Wales, and our governor-general Quentin Bryce among the guests. It was a big deal.

That day, we had a private family funeral for Uncle Ben, the type of funeral his parents would have wanted to be able to give him. It was a beautiful and emotional time for my mum and all the family in attendance.

At the time, the phone call from Brian confused me. It seemed out of character. Brian's job with the Australian Institute of Sport kept him away from home often for extended periods, including a four-week tour each year to France and England. We were used to being away from each other, and infidelity was not a concern in our relationship. We trusted each other implicitly.

It was not something I wanted to discuss with my mother, but I called a friend and asked them to check if Brian was okay.

Before the trip I had noticed some small changes in Brian which I had put down to fatigue from his work and study. Knowing what I know now, I suspect he had woken from a bad dream, and had begun to lose track of what was real and what was imagined.

At the time it was puzzling but it was the first real indication for me that something was wrong.

ONE

Inseparable

Dapto High School, 1973

I was 15 years old, in love with the idea of being in love and looking for a boyfriend and attention. Brian was 17, shy, studious and unbelievably good-looking.

I was sitting on the concrete steps of the school quadrangle, talking to my friend Bill and telling him how much I wished I could get Brian to talk to me. Bill got up, went over to Brian and brought him back.

'I am sick of listening to you moon over him,' Bill said to me. He turned to Brian: 'And I see you watching her all the time. Brian, this is Karen.' And Bill walked away. I still love Bill Dowson – no wonder!

Brian and I were inseparable from that day on.

On our first date, he drove his parents' car to pick me up. He wore a tie and collared shirt, and I had a new dress. After coming into our house and chatting to my father, who gave him my curfew, he walked to the passenger side of the car to open the door for me. Everything we knew about dating we had learned from watching American movies, and this seemed to be how it was done.

Brian took me to a Chinese restaurant in Windang, a nearby suburb. When we arrived at the restaurant and he pulled out a chair, I did too and sat down. He had to explain to me that he had pulled the chair out for me to sit on. I was so embarrassed I almost cried. I had never even smelled Chinese food before, so I ordered lamb chops and chips from the back of the menu while he ate a very exotic sweet-and-sour dish. I could not even contemplate eating something so foreign at the time. For years, he loved to tell his mates how unsophisticated I was on that date. I was 15! Before Brian drove me home, we went to a deserted car park by Lake Illawarra – so the date was not a complete disaster.

I honestly think it was a 'meeting of minds'. I was short and plain, and he was tall and handsome. We were both doing well in school and read voraciously, newspapers and books. We talked about politics, racism, the Vietnam War – things my friends thought boring. We were naïve in our opinions, as teenagers often are, but we did not know that then. I loved pop music and knew a bit about rugby league thanks to my father and brothers. Brian loved rugby league and knew a bit about pop music from his brother and sister.

It did help that our fathers were acquaintances – they knew each other from the local junior rugby league club, though Brian and I had not crossed paths before high school. As the years went on, our dads became best friends. My dad trusted Brian, as he knew his background, so I was allowed to go out with him. At 15, I wasn't allowed to go far, though. Brian had the same restrictions – his parents expected study on school nights.

Both of our families were obsessed with rugby league. My dad had always hoped that one or both of my brothers would play professionally. When that didn't happen, he was delighted that I had delivered the player of his dreams into the family through another door.

Brian and I had both grown up in Dapto, but on different sides of the town. We grew up in very similar families, though: happily married parents, and with three siblings each. Brian was the second of four children, between his older brother Allan and his younger sister Debbie. When Brian was 16 their youngest sister, Narelle, was born. She was the apple of everyone's eye!

Brian was studious and clever. After starting primary school in Dapto, he finished his last few years of primary in an opportunity class for gifted students in Wollongong. His main love was sport, though he always balanced it with other activities. As well as athletics and squash, he played rugby league from the age of seven, and I still have the Illawarra Under 12 Chess Champion trophy he won in 1967. He was also an air cadet, although I don't think he ever seriously considered joining the air force. By the time I met him, he had given it up, preferring instead to join his cousin Dale and crew on a sailing boat on Lake Illawarra every summer weekend.

In between all this, he was rarely found without a book in his hand. He loved adventure stories and thrillers – Alistair MacLean, John Le Carre, John Grisham and James Patterson. He was obsessed with the history of World Wars I and II and could tell you anything you wanted to know about any of the battles fought.

He always found time to mow his grandparents' lawn, help his father in the yard or with painting, and play with his adored baby sister. He had a part-time job working from 4 am each morning before school on the milk run, and after he turned 18 worked evenings as a drinks waiter at Dapto Leagues Club. Gosh, I make him sound like a saint – he did keep an extremely messy car full of old milkshake containers and chocolate wrappers! (Other than that, I think he was almost a saint.) He excelled in high school, especially in maths and sciences; he was the president of the student council and dux of Dapto High in 1974.

By then he was also playing rugby league in the senior divisions, at a time when country rugby league was in its heyday. He was one of the younger players in the Dapto team, who were lucky to be coached by former Australian rep Alan Fitzgibbon. Alan was without doubt Brian's first mentor: Brian admired him greatly and learned a lot about playing and coaching from him. At this time Brian was selected to represent Illawarra and later also represented NSW Country. This is where he came to the notice of the St George Dragons, and his professional rugby league career began.

After school, he started a science degree at the University of Wollongong, with no real plan for a career. But he found the study of science very dry and found himself gazing out the window during lectures, envying the students studying to be PE teachers at the teachers' college, which was also on the site. So, at the end of his first year of uni, he decided to join them, and swapped to a PE teaching degree.

It was one of the best decisions of his life. On his first day at teachers' college, he met the men who he always referred to as his brothers. I still refer to them as my brothers today. Brian loved teaching – though maybe not for all the right reasons. It was flexible enough to ensure he could play professional football, and if he was asked what he liked best about it, he always said it was the ten weeks' holiday every year.

During those years, I became the world's most dedicated girlfriend. I watched him sail, play football and squash, and mow lawns. I sat next to him, reading my own book, while he read his. My family adored him. I think my sister Jennifer, three years younger than me, was always a little in love with him too. My brothers – Ian, a year my junior, and Greg, five years younger – were both in awe of Brian's football prowess. Brian even coached a team that Greg played in as a teenager.

Brian was two years ahead of me at school, and although I too was doing well academically, I was terrified that he would go out into the big wide world of university and cease to be interested in a little schoolgirl. Much to my parents' and teachers' chagrin,

I left school and found a job as a receptionist at the end of Year 10. I studied part-time to learn typing and bookkeeping, which has always served me well.

We married in 1979, while Brian was in his last year of teacher training, on the only weekend available before he started to play for St George. He was 22, I was 20. We spent a blissful year living in a tiny flat in North Wollongong, not far from the beach, even though we had no money – Brian's football earnings would be paid in a lump sum at the end of the year. He was on a scholarship at teachers' college that paid $72 a month, and my take-home pay was $72 a week, leaving us with just enough for rent, food and petrol. We were surrounded in the neighbourhood by other students living as frugally as we were and partying hard. And we knew we would have extra income at the end of Brian's first footy season.

Thanks to rugby league, after that first year Brian and I had a much easier life than many of our friends. While our friends were going without restaurant dinners and holidays as they saved every penny for a house deposit, we were able to have a wonderful social life and pick up a deposit for our first home at the end of our first year of marriage.

I know that in marriage you need to get two of three major things right: financial stability, good communication and intimacy. We did not have to work hard on any of these things. Our financial stability was assured because of Brian's sports ability; we communicated beautifully – mainly because he was so easygoing and sensible; and the intimacy part was easy. We loved and trusted each other. There were never any major conflicts, and any minor conflicts were surmountable.

The biggest challenge we faced in our marriage was when we decided to start a family.

TWO

A family across the world

For eight long years, we tried to have a baby. It became an obsessive occupation for me, and Brian was my rock. We attempted IVF five times, always unsuccessfully. With the aid of fertility drugs, I feel pregnant 'naturally' eight times. Three of those pregnancies were ectopic. My wonderful gynaecologist saved my fallopian tube the first time, but the third ectopic almost killed me.

When Brian finished playing with St George in 1985, he was offered a playing position in England – in Warrington. Warrington is in Cheshire, about halfway between Manchester and Liverpool, and is about the same size as Wollongong. Brian suggested we take it up, just to take a break from trying to have a family.

We had always envied friends who had travelled through Europe, so decided it would be a working holiday. Brian would play for a year there, then we would spend anything he earned backpacking until the money ran out. Then we would come back to Australia and look at IVF again, or even overseas adoption.

The idea of a lifestyle change and a holiday appealed to us both. My health was not good at the time. I was incredibly unfit and had had nine surgeries in the previous 18 months – all related to infertility and miscarriage.

Brian took leave without pay from teaching, and I quit my job as a bank teller. We rented out our house and flew to Manchester. We had no idea what a turning point that 'working holiday' would be for our lives.

Brian loved the relaxed attitude of the Warrington Rugby League Club, and found the attitude of his English coach quite laissez faire in comparison to that of his St George coaches Harry Bath and Roy Masters. We had plenty of opportunity to travel through England, Scotland and Wales. He could miss a training night about once every two weeks and no one minded at all.

We were celebrities in the lovely village of Stockton Heath where we lived. Even an outing an hour down the road was an adventure for us. In the first three months we were there, we travelled to all the major northern English cities and to Scotland. I saw my first falling snow. I still remember the butterflies in my stomach as we exited the tube station and saw Trafalgar Square for the first time. Every day gave us a new experience or view. We were yet to conquer the local accents in a crowded pub, but we did eventually!

The other Australian and New Zealand players and their partners at Warrington during that time became our closest friends. In particular, Les and Judy Boyd and their two young children, Alicia and Grant, became like family to us. For me, they still are.

Les Boyd was a legend in rugby league at that time. He had come from a highly successful if controversial career in Sydney, and had represented Australia. I only knew of Les from reading the stories in Sydney newspapers, and when Brian told me he would be playing in the same team I did not imagine I would like him. For those who think Les is the hard man portrayed in those stories, I can assure you that he is not. He is a gentle, devoted family man and is kindness personified.

Although we had planned for Brian to play one year and then return to Australia after backpacking, our plans were thwarted when the nuclear reactor at Chernobyl exploded. Travel warnings for many of the areas we had planned to see on our backpacking trip were dire. The thought of drinking contaminated water was terrifying.

We took our money and headed to the US. It did not hold the same appeal, though, and when the Eastern Suburbs Roosters club contacted Brian, we dropped our travel plans and headed home to Sydney for him to play for the rest of the 1986 season.

Our first year had been so good that when Brian was offered a second season at Warrington, we did not think twice about taking up the offer. Our friends the Boyds were also returning, and our European travel plans were back on the agenda.

During that second year, I watched a BBC program on the problems of finding parents for children with special needs or of mixed race in Britain. I was astounded that prospective parents with infertility problems would be at all choosy about which babies to adopt, and started to investigate adoption in England.

It was not without its hurdles. A couple of non-resident foreigners wanting to legally adopt a British citizen was a new challenge for the Children's Services department of our local council. Luckily, they were intrigued by our application and up for the challenge.

I don't mean to gloss over the details of this and make it sound easy. It was quite arduous, but like any fairy tale it had a happy ending. Once we jumped the hurdles and our application was accepted, we spent almost every spare moment during the 1986 English rugby league season devoted to interviews, medicals, criminal checks and parenting classes.

At the end of the league season we packed up our tent and sleeping bags and toured Europe for eight weeks. What an adventure that was! We put our adoption hopes to one side, expecting a long wait. We relaxed. The holiday through France, Italy, Greece, the former Yugoslavia, Germany, Austria, Switzerland and Belgium was everything we had wanted it to be.

My birthday – 20 July 1987 – was a significant day. Brian telephoned Warrington Council from Athens to confirm our acceptance as suitable adoptive parents. I was so nervous I stayed in our room, staring at the Acropolis in the distance, while Brian made the call from the foyer of our hotel. He almost broke through the door to hug me and tell me of the positively joyous outcome of that call. Being the calm and sensible man he was, he also told me to expect a long wait.

We followed the eight-week camping trip with a flight home to Australia to visit family, and while staying with my parents in Dapto were gobsmacked to get a phone call from Warrington Council telling us to come back straightaway. A baby had been placed in their care; the adoption board and his biological mother were considering our application.. He was already waiting for us.

We rushed back to England on the next available flight. It was at Heathrow that our plans began to unravel.

Brian and I headed to the immigration desk together and he presented his passport first; it had a work permit and so was duly stamped. I handed my passport to the immigration officer and she asked why I was in England. I answered simply, 'I'm with him', and smiled at her. She did not smile back.

I had somehow neglected to pay about $35 to the British Government as the spouse of someone with a work visa. My passport was confiscated, and I was almost deported back to Australia. Lots of tears later, lots of bureaucracy, the intervention of our local MP, leave to remain in the country for three days, a flight to Belgium and some red tape eventually saw the problem fixed – but not without more stress than I thought we could cope with.

On 18 August 1987, a Tuesday morning, we purchased all the baby supplies people usually stockpile over nine months. That afternoon, we met and bathed our son.

On Wednesday morning, we became parents when Brett Alan

Johnson, aged six weeks and perfect in every way, was delivered to our arms.

I remember distinctly our first night with our new baby in the next room. We stayed awake all night, holding hands and listening to every gurgle and whimper he made. Brian turned to me in the morning and said, 'I know it's been hard – but aren't you glad we have had nine years together before we had a baby?' I had to agree. Infertility had become almost an obsessive occupation for me. It had created physical pain for me and mental pain for both of us. We hated the uncertainty, and not being able to fulfil our dreams of having a family. That all dissolved with Brett's arrival.

Brian deeply fell in love the minute he held Brett in his arms. At the pre-adoption hearing, our solicitor had asked what we would do if the court said we could not move back to Australia with the baby. 'No problem,' Brian said, 'we'll stay here. And if they say we can only keep him if we move to Iceland, then we are moving to Iceland in the morning.'

Adoption is not a cure for infertility. Yearning to have a baby is biological. You need to have stopped wanting to be pregnant before you are ready to adopt. Brian and I were sick of trying to conceive. Brett was our son, a result of what we called our eight-year labour.

The planned one-year working holiday had already changed the course of our lives. It also changed the trajectory of Brian's career.

Our two years in England became three when Brian decided to play for another season. When he was offered the job of head coach at Warrington, we stayed on.

Two years after Brett's adoption, we applied to adopt a second child. We did not hear anything for three years and had almost given up hope when an unexpected phone call in October 1992 heralded the arrival of our second son, Liam Samuel Johnson.

We both fell deeply in love again. Even now the boys are adults, I am still waiting to be tapped on the shoulder by someone saying they made a mistake, and we weren't qualified to adopt them after all.

Brian was always a wonderful and attentive dad, and was lucky to have a career with flexible hours. When Brett was a baby, Brian was playing for Warrington so was home with us during the day until he went to training sessions in the evening.

In fact, on the day Brett arrived home with us, Brian was the first to change him. When it was obvious that a nappy change was required, I reached for the nappy bag, relishing my role as a traditional mum. But Brian took it from my hand. 'I am doing this,' he said. 'If I don't get my hands dirty today, I may never be able to do it.' From then on, he never had a problem with dirty nappies or vomit where small children were concerned.

He was there for Brett's first words, his first step, his first day at nursery, his first nativity play, his first day at school. He attended every school awards day, school play and concert. By the time Liam arrived, Brian was coaching at Warrington, so his work was a little less flexible. But he made sure he was around for all the 'firsts' in Liam's life too. As Liam grew up, he and Brian developed a special bond. They became best mates.

Brian stayed coaching at Warrington for seven years. At one stage, he was the longest serving current coach in British rugby league. He was also the youngest. In his years there, the team won the Lancashire Cup and the Regal Trophy, and he took the club to the Challenge Cup final at Wembley in 1990, their first appearance there in many years. They didn't win but at the celebration dinner afterwards you wouldn't have guessed that. It was the highlight of his career. One of his proudest moments was driving through the local village of Latchford and seeing the words 'We all march in Johnson's army' spray-painted on the two-storey wall of a local building.

As a coach, Brian was highly successful – until he wasn't. But that is the normal career path of a rugby league coach. You can be flavour of the month for a while, and then you get the sack.

We returned to Australia in 1996, and settled into an ordinary Australian life: living in the suburbs of Wollongong, volunteering on school canteens, taking Brett and Liam to sports and their other interests, both of us taking up new studies and moving into new jobs.

Brian's jobs were still exciting, though. Although he briefly went back to teaching at a local high school, his heart was still in rugby league, and after his successful years at Warrington he wanted to build on his coaching career. He landed a role as football manager with the Western Suburbs Magpies; Tom Raudonikis was coach, and Brian had hoped to find an opening there on the coaching staff. Then an opportunity came up to work with Ron Hilditch at the Parramatta Eels, and Brian volunteered his services. He became assistant coach to Ron shortly afterwards. He was kept on a as assistant coach to Brian Smith, then moved to the Illawarra Steelers as reserve grade coach, in 1998 taking that team to the only grand final win that the Steelers ever achieved before they were incorporated into the St George club.

Head coach roles in the Australian Rugby League (ARL) are few and far between, and when Brian heard of the new proposed joint effort between the Australian Institute of Sport and the ARL for a program for elite young players in Canberra, he applied. His coaching experience combined with his teaching background made him an excellent choice for the job. It was a groundbreaking program and, as the first person in that position, Brian had many ideas and the contacts he needed to organise annual overseas tours in France and England. Bob Millward, the esteemed director of the

St George Illawarra Dragons, once introduced Brian at a dinner as 'our first Professor of Rugby League'.

Brian's dedication to the set-up, management, administration and coaching as the head coach of rugby league at the AIS was unwavering. He coached players such as Israel Folau, Kodi Nicareema, Chris Sandow, Ewan Aitken, Blake Ferguson and Curtis Scott, to name a few. At the same time, he decided to study part-time at the University of Wollongong for his Master of Business Administration (MBA).

Brian poured an enormous number of hours into his role at the AIS, so when I started to notice him becoming a little disorganised, I thought it was fatigue. Perhaps he just needed to slow down a little, I thought. But it soon became clear that something else was going on.

THREE

Road to diagnosis

In 2000, about four years after we returned to Australia, Brian joined some of his oldest mates for a weekend in Mollymook, on the NSW South Coast, to play golf. They played at a course called Hilltop.

He came home from that trip, threw his clubs into the garage in anger and said he would never play golf again. He blamed his friend, the late English golf pro Mike Slater, for his fading ability. 'Bloody Mike Slater!' he told me. 'I have been crap since he gave me lessons!'

Brian had never been a great golfer, though his hand–eye coordination was superb. But he did love the game, and played regularly and keenly with his friends. He was competitive in everything he did and although he was not a gambler, he and his best mates played for high stakes on the golf course: a Cherry Ripe chocolate bar on each hole. Brian *loved* Cherry Ripes, so he played to win every time.

But on the Mollymook trip, he just could not hit a ball from a tee. The club *always* connected with the ground just behind the ball, leaving a divot and causing hilarity among his playing partners. They renamed the course on that trip, and still refer to it as 'Flattop' when they retell the story.

From that point, Brian really did give up golf. He would occasionally play with me or be coerced to join a group of mates, but he became so frustrated and angry when playing that he no longer enjoyed it. Looking back, this is the first major thing I remember changing for Brian. It would be another decade before he was diagnosed with dementia.

It was around the same time as the golfing trip, in 2001, that Brian decided to return to university to work towards an MBA, studying just one subject at a time to fit it in with his full-time work. He started with great enthusiasm and knocked over the first few subjects very quickly but, as the course progressed, he complained that he was getting too old to study and could not hold information in his head.

He plugged away slowly at the course so as not to waste the money he had spent on it, and in 2008 withdrew early, receiving a Master of Management instead of the MBA he had set out to achieve. For all his doubts, he gained distinctions in every subject. He vowed never to study again, though – something he had always found easy – as it had become too hard.

By then, I had started to notice some differences in Brian too. He was only in his late forties but seemed to be less interested in his work, a bit forgetful with names and dates, and a little complacent about his dress and shaving. I seemed to take over a lot of his traditional roles at home – disciplining the children, making decisions about our finances, organising outings. Not that he had always done all those things before; he just seemed to defer to me for final decisions. A lot of these traits reminded me of his father, and I was happy to accept the changes – at first. He did not discuss any concerns he had with me about these things.

I noticed a difference in his driving, too. He had always been a careful and thoughtful driver. I was the one who would flout the rules. One evening, he drove Brett home to Shellharbour, to the house he shared with friends, 20 minutes away. As soon as Brian had dropped him off, Brett, who has never had a driver's licence, telephoned me. He had been terrified by Brian's driving on the 12-kilometre trip. He said he had to tell Brian to 'Pick a lane, Dad!' all the way up the highway. He had thought his dad was playing some sort of silly prank, which was very out of character, and he was concerned. It was one more sign that something wasn't right.

He had always been an early riser – a result, he said, of working on the milk run as a high school student – and he would be out of bed every morning at about 4.30 am to begin his day. In days gone by, he would exercise early and get ready to go to work.

But when he began to work from our home office, only travelling to the Australian Institute of Sport in Canberra or to his desk at the Australian Rugby League in Sydney when he needed to, he started to skip the getting-ready-for-work bit. I suppose there was a decline in his grooming that was so gradual I didn't really notice. It did not matter to me if he did not shave for a few days, or wore clothes that were mismatched when he was only staying in the office at home. I just did the usual wifey nag if we were going out, and he would comply and tidy himself up.

Brian had never been interested in clothes anyway. Like so many of his footballing mates (and young men in general, I think), he loved a free T-shirt with a logo, a pair of comfortable shorts and thongs. He had, however, always been scrupulously clean and well aware of how to dress for work and special occasions. Only one member of our family had a wardrobe budget – and I took that right very seriously!

I remember one Dally M Awards ceremony in particular, in 1981. It was in the days before WAGS ('wives and girlfriends') wore designer gowns and borrowed diamond jewellery. I am sure Brian commented, 'What's wrong with the dress you wore last year?' when I suggested I might buy something new. He did not own a dinner suit, nor did any of his teammates, so he hired a black tux for the night. And he only owned one pair of good leather shoes – they were black – so, getting ready for the night, he reached into the wardrobe, pulled out two shoes, did up the laces and off we went.

The function that year was held in Sydney Tower. We were going down in the lift at the end of the night with some other couples from St George when his teammate, Tony Trudgett, pointed at Brian's shoes and started laughing. A few weeks before, Brian had been a groomsman at a friend's wedding, and worn a brown top hat, tails, and a pair of his brother's brown shoes borrowed for the occasion. Now, to the Dally M Awards, he had managed to wear one black and one brown shoe. He thought it was hilarious. He certainly wasn't concerned that anyone might have noticed.

Brian noticed that things were changing for him long before he confided in me about his concerns. In 2009, he visited his doctor because he felt 'woolly-headed', later telling me that he felt like he was moving through thick fog sometimes. He read a book that suggested his forgetfulness might be a side effect of his cholesterol medication. He gave them up. He tried taking Vitamin D tablets, krill oil, CoQ10 and multivitamins. He had also begun to experience a tremor, and small but uncontrollable jerks in his arms and legs.

Brian dealt with this quietly. He would have thought he was protecting me from unnecessarily worrying until he knew exactly what was going on. He obviously did not understand it himself and perhaps even thought he was imagining some of his symptoms. It was his way to deal in facts; he liked to solve problems, not speculate on them. Initially, I did not know he was seeing his GP.

The following year, I travelled to Europe with my mother for three weeks, and in Bruges received the phone call from Brian that I found so concerning. On my return home, a very unkempt Brian met me at the airport and announced that he had become a vegetarian. This knocked my socks off! How could a man who loved steaks, chops and sausages as much as he did just give them up? However, I needed to lose some weight, and I did not want to prepare two different meals each evening, so I happily became a vegetarian with him.

He remained a vegetarian for about five weeks, then forgot all about it. It was kind of fun cooking different meals during that time, though we both ended up craving rare fillet steak and moved back to our old diet easily.

Luckily Brian's GP, Dr Jones, took his concerns seriously. He ran a barrage of tests and prescribed some supplements.

We knew Dr Jones socially, a little, through his work as the club doctor for the Dragons, and I regularly dealt with him in my work as a human resources administrator. One day, when I was accompanying a colleague with a workers compensation claim, Dr Jones asked my colleague to wait outside while he spoke to me. I thought he was about to tell me my colleague was faking a back injury but was taken aback when he mentioned Brian. He could not give me details due to confidentiality rules, but he asked me to make a new appointment for Brian and to attend with him.

He was surprised to find out that I knew so little about Brian's concerns, and he stressed how important it was for Brian and me to talk about what was happening. He wanted me to attend all Brian's appointments from then on, as he had noticed how uncharacteristically dishevelled Brian was becoming and how he did not remember from one appointment to the next what they had talked about. 'Karen, he comes to my office and looks like he has left his brown paper bag with the wine flagon in it in the car,' Dr Jones said. From that moment on, I became properly involved in Brian's health.

Dr Jones researched the best neurologists and wrote a referral for a renowned specialist in Sydney. We visited him three times.

On the first trip, Brian drove while I navigated. We had never been to the suburb before, and I had no idea his driving had become so bad. It had been a long time since he had driven in Sydney traffic and he became confused making a right-hand turn at a set of lights. When the light changed to amber, then red, he remained halfway through the turn in the middle of the road, with car horns blaring at him and me yelling at him to 'Turn the bloody corner!' He pulled over in tears a few metres up the road. He just could not work out what the problem had been, but he knew that he should have been able to work it out.

We arrived at the neurologist's office a few minutes later, shaken but able to put the incident behind us.

On our third visit, the neurologist gave us the diagnosis we had been dreading.

Dear Dr Y.,

I wish I had understood about neurologists when we came to see you.

We were sent to you by a very caring GP who had heard you were the best. You certainly knew how to schedule all the tests.

But you are just clever. You are not about care. We did not know that.

You had a lovely, friendly manner when we saw you. Pictures on the wall showed you with rugby players and other celebrities. You listened to all our concerns and watched Brian walk up the room. You checked his tremor. You conducted a cognitive test that my clever husband found incredibly difficult. Brian and I laughed about it later – about how he was so nervous that he could not even do such a simple test.

You organised blood tests, brain scans and a lumbar puncture. You made us feel like the things we described were normal and maybe stress related. I felt like you dismissed some things I talked about.

The lumbar puncture sounded like a big deal but the hospital made it feel routine. Brian had to remain prone in bed for four hours after the needle, so I went shopping. They said he might get a headache. He did not.

So the next day he drove to St Marys Leagues Stadium in Sydney to watch a schoolboys' rugby league tournament. He called me from St Marys to say he would be home about 6 pm.

I do not remember why but I came home early, about 2 pm, to find his car in the drive. When I came inside, I found him in bed, and when I woke him he was frighteningly sick. He did not know where he was or how he got there. He could barely speak. He had a horrible headache and seemed to be hallucinating.

I called your office. You were not available. I called an ambulance. You never called me back.

Brian's problems settled down in Wollongong Hospital, where they nodded and told us it was a common reaction to a lumbar puncture. I wish I had known. I cannot understand how he drove home in that condition without having or causing an accident.

Our next visit started out as friendly as them all. You went through all the tests. Told us he did not have HIV or syphilis. Then you said his brain was atrophied. That he had dementia, Alzheimer's type. That he had an expected life span of about six more years. Then you sat back with an 'Aren't I clever for diagnosing that?' smile and folded your arms.

We were shocked.

You said nothing more. You ushered us out of the office. You did not offer one word of advice. Not even a brochure with the phone number of Alzheimer's Australia on it. Not another appointment. Nothing.

No care. No solace. No direction.

I do not remember what it cost to see you but the trappings of your office showed that your work is lucrative. Can't you afford to put in at least a brochure stand with some basic information leaflets, or train your receptionist to tell us who to go to next?

I was recently told that neurologists are not part of the care plan for dementia patients. Okay. I understand that now. But you need to know that when you give someone a death sentence, getting rid of them from your office is not good enough.

After that appointment, Brian seemed to shut down. He told me not to speak about it to anyone. We drove home in silence.

FOUR

Life goes on

After Brian's diagnosis, life carried on.

I was forbidden by Brian to tell anyone what the neurologist had told us. He became convinced he could fix this problem with diet and vitamins, or that a cure for dementia was imminent and he would have the cure before anyone needed to know. He began to read about neuroplasticity. His plan was to train the healthy part of his brain to take over from the parts already affected and all would be okay.

He read that turmeric was a miracle cure. I read that it was based on research on dementia sufferers whose diets already included a lot of turmeric. I also read that you would have to ingest copious amounts of it for it to make a difference. I thought it was another pointless 'snake oil'. Brian was furious with me for doubting his research. I know it is available now in Australia but back then I had to import turmeric tea in a box of 1000 bags and it was expensive. It took a month to arrive. Brian did not drink any sort of tea or coffee, but he planned to drink his turmeric tea at least three times a day and he would be fine.

I brewed him a cup. He sniffed it, said it smelled like dirt, took one sip and spat it out. I threw out 999 turmeric tea bags about six months later.

If we did not tell anyone of his diagnosis, Brian thought, then no one would even notice.

I was not so convinced.

Despite all the signs and symptoms, I still had not expected the devastating diagnosis of dementia. My husband, my rock, refused to discuss anything about it. He became angry with me if I tried to talk about our future or any arrangements that might need to be made. I wanted to cry and be held and be comforted while I also comforted him. I needed to come up with strategies. Brian refused to believe it would happen to him; for him it was a dirty little secret and not to be mentioned.

Family, friends and Brian's workmates sometimes commented on the little things he did, and I had to lie and brush off their concerns. I felt isolated. I had no one to talk to.

I went to see my GP in tears. He was very up to date on local support for younger onset dementia (YOD) and put me in touch with a care provider, Community Options, that had just begun to offer a local support group for YOD. I wasn't sure if I could make use of a group that Brian refused to become involved in, but I had to reach out for some support, even if I did it secretly. So, when Brian was travelling in France with his AIS rugby league team, I went to a support group on my own. It was a new group; we were all meeting for the first time.

A group of about 20 people, some carers and some suffering from various types of dementia, sat in a circle in a private room at a lovely Wollongong restaurant with a view of the ocean. The convenor asked us to introduce ourselves and say a little about why we were there.

The man on my right was the first to speak. Then it was my turn, and I could do nothing but sob. They moved on and when they came back to me half an hour later, I was still crying. The stories of everyone in the room were heartbreaking. I cried for them a little. I cried for me a lot.

I did manage to tell my story, though, and over time I gained a lot of information and strength from that support group. Never underestimate how important it is to have people around you with empathy for your situation. When you are lost, they give you somewhere to start, with ways to cope and information to research, and the confidence to know that what you are feeling is authentic. Talking about what you have learned from your own problems and experiences helps others too. They remind you that you are never completely alone.

Brian returned from his annual trip to France embarrassed about how much help he had needed from his assistant coaches. He had done the same trip every year for nine years with a different team of young players, and it had an entrenched routine. Everything was scheduled to the hour, if not the minute, so Brian could manage it with the help of his assistant coaches. The management team included a doctor who had become one of Brian's good friends. Brian had confided in him, and I had spoken to 'the doc', and the coaches who had worked side by side with Brian for years, about his extra needs. All were prepared to help, and they did.

Some months after that trip Brian and I had a long conversation about how hard his life was becoming. I would come home from work to find the floors of our house covered in little piles of printed A4 paper as Brian struggled to collate the booklets he would put together for his players. He constantly 'lost' files in the computer and I would come home from work to find them for him. He blamed everyone in our house for stealing his office equipment. He would just buy more staplers or hole punches when he could not find his usual one. I still have eight staplers on the desk today. He would throw away printers and shredders that he said had stopped working, then buy new ones. It took about three replacement printers in a month for me to realise it was not the printers that had the problem.

He decided he needed to resign his position. He could not do the day-to-day work, and I was becoming too tired to cope – after a busy day at work, I would come home to begin the administration work of his program.

I called the then-CEO at Australian Rugby League and gave him an outline of the problems before I put a very tearful Brian on the phone. He refused to accept Brian's resignation, and called a meeting of officials and coaches from the ARL and AIS at our house the following week.

Basically, they asked him why he would want to give up his salary when they could put support in place for him to continue. This was so unexpected. To this day I have never heard of another employer taking these steps to assist anyone with dementia in the workplace. We were extremely lucky that Brian held the position he held and was not a plant operator on a construction site – or, for that matter, still a schoolteacher. There are very few jobs that can be modified safely for someone with dementia to continue working.

In my experience, dementia changes the brain incrementally every day. A normal job would need to be modified every day to keep up with the lost abilities of a worker with dementia. Someone with a brain injury or a disability can do a modified job because their abilities remain the same, day by day. But dementia slowly chips away at your abilities. Something you can still do in the morning can be gone from you by the evening – especially, it seems, in younger onset dementia. The brain changes more rapidly than you can imagine.

Part of Brian's job was to be the figurehead of the program he initiated and designed. He was held in high esteem by both organisations that oversaw his work. In particular, Brian's colleagues David Norman and Peter O'Sullivan were invaluable. They kept a close eye on Brian and his workload. They accompanied him on overseas trips and gave me the confidence to let Brian continue working, because I knew David and Peter were not only helping but also protecting him.

Through the wonderful support of his colleagues, and the hierarchy of the AIS and the ARL, Brian was able to continue working. It assisted greatly with his self-esteem and was also a great comfort to me that Brian did not abruptly lose his career and his worth. This kindness gave us much more than just his continuing salary.

Brian had always been very modest about his achievements in the sport of rugby league. I recall him saying once that he hoped he did not become one of the old player types sitting on the stool at the pub and regaling everyone with the details of how many tries he'd scored.

Now, at work, his team of elite young players were less likely to understand what was happening to him and why he did some of the things he did. As he became aware of things slipping away from him, he was worried that the new intake of players – aged 16 to 18 – who had never seen him play would think he did not know what he was talking about. He felt that he needed to justify his position at work, so he had a DVD made that showed a series of his tries and long spectacular runs from his playing career. It became part of the induction session into the AIS program, and he also showed it on the TV screen on the team bus. He would hand a copy to anyone who would take one. He just wanted to be the person he had always been.

Although his colleagues were for the most part a wonderful help to him, I wanted Brian to leave work with his dignity intact. He pleaded with me to agree to one last trip to France and England. For him to do this, his best friend, Garry Posetti, went with him. Garry had also worked in rugby league as a strength and conditioning coach with both the Parramatta Eels and the Illawarra Steelers, so he was more than qualified for a role on the trip.

Knowing Garry was with him assuaged my anxiety as well. Had I anticipated some of the stories I heard on their return, though, I would not have let him go that last year. One of those stories was how he was 'lost' for two hours or so in the Manchester Christmas markets. I know now that Garry was very close to making a dreaded phone call to me when Brian popped out of a crowd asking where the hell everyone had been. Phew! On his return from that trip, Brian was easily persuaded to retire. He finished working in 2013.

One of the directors at the Australian Institute of Sport rang and asked about the type of function Brian would like as a send-off. It could be formal or casual, and would be attended by all the players in his current AIS rugby league team, the new head coach taking over from him, representatives of AIS management, and all the people who had worked with him on the program for the previous 13 years. I asked for finger food and tracksuit pants; Brian was beyond cutlery and formal clothes at that stage. They organised a function with sandwiches and sausage rolls, and Brian came in his AIS sports uniform without looking out of place. There were several speeches and a presentation, and Brian was expected to reply.

Brian and I discussed how he wanted to respond. His language skills had declined so much by then that such a public speech would have been impossible for him to manage. It was not something I was used to doing, but on that day I spoke for him. He was presented with a beautiful glass trophy commemorating his work. He stood beside me and I held his hand tightly as I thanked everyone on his behalf. His team rose spontaneously at the end and gave him a round of applause.

I continued working for a few months after that, sometimes taking Brian into work with me for a few hours, where he would pace through my workplace until my colleagues were tired of it. Mostly he stayed at home alone. If I could, I would drive home at lunchtime or arrange for a friend or for his sister Narelle to call on him to break up his day. The company I worked for was also wonderful, understanding that my changing circumstances needed flexibility, and they did what they could to support me.

I resisted giving up my job even when I knew things were becoming too hard for Brian. I just wanted to believe that life could be tweaked a little, then go on as normal. One evening I came in from work and he was waiting for me by the front door. He told me he was too scared to be on his own, and that he couldn't even manage to eat the lunch I had left prepared for him. He needed me to stay with him every day.

I arrived at my office the next morning to explain to my CEO that I had to give as short a notice as they would take. He told me that he had anticipated it and I could leave that day but a job would be waiting for me if I decided to return to work. It made my departure feel as supported as my position had been. Luckily my accumulated annual leave and long service leave would keep us going for a while until we could negotiate the welfare system. Again, the case manager from our service provider stepped in to help us to apply for the payments we were soon entitled to.

Brian had worked from the age of 14. I had only been without a job while we lived in England. This was a new world for us. We had to find ways to be occupied, together.

Our new group of friends from the YOD support group were all about the same age as us, ranging from about 48 to 64. They were a mix of men and women with different diseases, but the commonality was that those diseases were atrophying their brains. We met regularly for coffee and picnics and socialised at each other's homes. Sometimes the partner with dementia would be agitated and angry with their partner. I learned quickly that distraction could relieve their agitation, and the group was very intuitive about who might need to 'swap' partners for a period of socialising.

Brian was offered a social outing with a men's group who attended the gym together with paid carers. A bus picked them up, they went to a gym for exercise, finished with a coffee and were returned by bus. At first he was horrified and refused to attend. He felt like he was being put on a bus with the 'special kids' and thought he might run into old rugby league mates in the gym. He carried a terrible, unwarranted shame about his condition.

I do not know how I tricked him into going the first time – I know I drove him to the gym, and he did not get picked up by the bus. What a revelation it was to him: a normal group of men in a private but normal gym who exercised while joking around. He needed a bit of help to use some of the machines, but he was in his old familiar world. They even held a competition to see who could go the furthest on the rowing machine. Of course Brian won that!

He could discuss the problems of dementia with these men, and they quickly bonded. He looked forward to their biweekly session, and he did not need to tell his old friends about this new group at all.

It was hard for Brian to step into the unknown. He had always been a remarkable athlete. He was brilliant at maths and science at school. He was dux of our high school. He achieved his teaching diploma easily and with distinction. He even completed his master's degree with dementia beginning to eat away at his brain. He was held in high regard as a teacher, a rugby league player, a rugby league coach and an administrator.

Becoming disabled and finding the activities of daily living difficult in what we saw as the prime of our lives was never anticipated. Not by either of us.

Dear Brian,

Today we had a fight. Fighting isn't something we do very often and, as usual, five minutes after it was over we were both apologising and having a cuddle. It really is my fault, though. I am so intolerant of the little things. The things I know shouldn't matter seem to take over my world.

You wanted to help me hang out the washing.

Once you started working from home – about 13 years ago – you took over doing the washing. It was much easier than me trying to fit it in before and after work or on weekends. Now you feel like I have stolen a job off you – something you could always do – and you tell everyone that now I won't let you do it, and that I think you're useless. I know it makes you mad.

It was one of the first things I noticed about the effects of dementia on your ability to plan and problem-solve. Who would have thought we needed planning and problem-solving skills to hang out the washing! You couldn't sort the colours from the whites; you couldn't work out where to turn the dial on the machine to start the cycle; you kept lifting your head under the clothesline and cutting your scalp on the supports; you hung clothes by one peg, secured anywhere on the garment, and stretched it; you hung dirty clothes on the line; you dropped freshly washed clothes on the ground and stood on them; you forgot to hang them out at all; you brought in wet clothes immediately after they had been hung out; you carried the basket to the line and forgot why you were there …

I know I should let you do it anyway and then fix it later – and I have tried to do that – but you get so frustrated and upset it just doesn't seem worth it at all. I hate setting you up to fail and most of the time I am so tired that the thought of redoing a job makes me want to cry.

Today you were just jamming pegs on the line without any clothes attached to them. You thought you were helping, so I let you get on with that and hung the clothes myself. When I was finished, you were so cross with me for not allowing you to help that you stormed off into the house.

You told me that I have to let you practise so you can get better at it. I can't explain to you that your brain is withering away and taking even the smallest of your skills with it. You think you are beating this hideous disease and I cannot tell you that you are not.

I am so sorry for being so intolerant. I want to be the saintly carer that people seem to think I am, but I am just an inadequate and selfish wife who just wants her clever, strong husband back.

FIVE

Home and away

After his diagnosis, Brian and I talked about how we would cope. Perhaps the most important thing we decided was that we would not do depression in our house. We made a pact to look for the joy in our days, no matter how small, and focus on that.

We did that together. We laughed and we loved until he died. That's not to say we didn't cry. We cried. A lot.

Brian was incredibly stoic about his diagnosis. He tried not to dwell on it, wanting to still be my protector. Only once, when I was trying to lighten a frustrating moment for him, did he completely lose his cool and chastise me. I don't remember what I said, but one morning when something innocuous happened (perhaps he pulled a sock from the drawer instead of a baseball cap), I made a joke about it. He was suddenly really angry with me. 'Do you think what is happening to me is funny?' he shouted. 'How can you laugh at me?' He stormed from the room, leaving me in tears. For an hour, I cried alone in the bedroom while he ranted to no one downstairs.

I am sure we resolved it amicably before the day finished but I never again joked when he did something silly. Even now, when I think of it, I still feel a stab of shame that I hurt him so much.

Almost everyone I have met who has been given a diagnosis that may be terminal does two things. They get expensive family portraits done, and they go on the holiday of a lifetime. Our beautiful family portrait hangs in the dining room where I see it every time I come down the stairs. In it, Brian is hugging me to him, as he always did, as we stand between our beautiful sons.

In March 2011, our 32nd wedding anniversary, we organised what we jokingly referred to as our 'last big holiday' and had the equivalent of a honeymoon in Tahiti. No expense was spared. It was a truly romantic and relaxing holiday, and we had no major dramas – except for finding out on a busy road that Brian had forgotten how to balance when riding a bicycle.

I wish I had a photograph of poor Brian's predicament. He fell into a deep, newly dug drainage ditch on the side of the road, with his bike straddling the ditch and a wheel on each side of the hole, while he was suspended under the bike and hanging on for dear life. He was a bit upset with me, as I had persuaded him to ride the bike – but we were on a second honeymoon, so he forgave me quickly, and in hindsight we laughed about it. It was a great story for Brian to tell his best mates on our return, when he could paint me as the villain. Some strongly built Tahitian roadworkers were on hand to haul him out – he did look hilarious, but they did not laugh at all while we were there. We chained the bikes to a pole and continued on our way on foot.

At the end of the next year, we felt so good we had a second 'last big holiday' – to Switzerland with friends, then onto Alaska. We faced some challenges and made some adjustments, but I think we just seemed like a quirky couple to most of our fellow travellers. Brian became very angry with me as I helped with the first meal served to us on the flight. It took some explaining to calm him down but, as usual, he eventually saw sense and trusted me to help him.

Over the years, I had watched many women collect their husband's meals at buffets. I had always assured Brian that I would never turn into 'her'. But I don't look at women or men who wait hand and foot on their partners with contempt anymore. They could just be trying to maintain their partners' dignity, as I was. So I really did not care if people thought I was a 'subservient' wife who did everything for her 'lazy' husband.

Brian and I had been lucky enough throughout our time together to be able to afford some fantastic holidays. Some of the holidays we experienced in our twenties and thirties are the sort that people spend their whole working lives planning to do once they retire.

Our first holiday together was the year after we had both left school, staying in a rundown caravan near Brisbane. It was the very first time I had been beyond the Sydney Harbour Bridge. The Polaroid photos we took on that trip show two happy teenagers. I think that was the last time Brian comfortably swam in the ocean for the rest of his life – his shark phobia was legendary among his friends.

Our first overseas trip together was to Hawaii, and while we lived in England we travelled in the US and extensively in Europe. We filled dozens of albums with photographs over the ten years we were there. Once the boys arrived, our trips changed a little. Our two-man tent became a much larger one with a kitchen set-up, and our wanderings included Disneyland and water parks. We went with other families. Our holidays slowed down so that the boys had time to spend with other children. It all became more relaxed.

Once we returned to Australia in 1996, we bought an onsite caravan at Lake Conjola on the NSW South Coast, where we boated, swam, barbecued and socialised. We also fitted in trips to the Gold Coast for days spent at theme parks, which delighted not only Brett and Liam but Brian too.

We also discovered skiing. When Brian had been a professional rugby league player, skiing was not something we had ever considered. As well as it being another winter sport, which meant we did not have the time to ski, the risk of injury was just too great for a professional player.

Brian took to it with his usual enthusiasm, and his natural coordination meant he picked it up quickly. In 2008, after several joint family holidays with our friends, we purchased a ski club membership in Jindabyne.

This was just as Brian's abilities were beginning to decline. The biggest problem for him at the start was constantly misplacing equipment. I spent just as much time sorting out Brian's gloves and goggles as I had done for the children when they were younger. He would pull his ski gloves off without paying attention to the lining and I would spend ten minutes having to push the wet lining back into the fingers of his gloves. I'd just get it fixed and he would do it again. I gave up expecting him to look after his gloves, goggles and helmet. It was easier to carry it all myself than to buy new ones every day.

The coordination of his equipment and getting his ski boots on were a huge frustration, but his muscle memory was still wonderful and, once dressed, he would take off downhill as he always had.

On the last trip we did there together, in 2013, I stopped as usual to hire our boots and skis in Jindabyne. I helped fit Brian's boots and was carrying our gear to the car when one of the sales assistants stopped me at the door. She handed me a card for volunteers who ski with the disabled. I was, as usual, trying to keep our life normal and I thought I was covering for him so well no one would notice. Apparently, we stood out like sore thumbs. But what a wonderful organisation! It was not something that I felt we could use but I am delighted to know it exists and is so thoughtfully promoted.

We headed up to Perisher on the first morning and did a chair ride together on the Village Eight to the top of the beginners' run, just to get our ski legs. We skied off the chair with no problems and Brian beat me to the bottom of the hill. He looked smooth and turned beautifully, as usual.

I caught up with him at the bottom and we again queued for the chairlift. He managed to shuffle forward into a space on the chair ahead of the one we had originally queued together for and suddenly he was not beside me. I watched him sit on the chair without a problem and hoped he could get off without my prompting.

Unfortunately, he did not get off the chair when everyone else did. He was still sitting on it as it turned to go back down the hill – so he jumped. He ended up under the lift, on the wrong side of the pylon in a ditch. Of course, the chair had to stop and I was stranded on the chair behind him, unable to help or explain to his rescuers. They managed to get him and his gear into the right place without any great drama or injury. I came off the chair and skied over to him.

Of course he believed it was my fault, and he let me have it with both barrels for not being on the chair with him. I told him that I was through with skiing, and that I would get arrested for putting a vulnerable person in danger. We both calmed down a little and I was attempting to get him to put his booted foot onto the ski when a 'helpful' skier came over to explain to us that people without any ski ability should not be on that hill and we could get lessons at the base. He even suggested we take our skis off and walk back down to ensure our safety.

I thanked him politely and tried to make it look like I was heeding his advice. Inside my head, I was chanting, 'Fuck off, fuck off, just fuck off!' I hoped my eyes did not give me away.

We skied competently to the bottom of the hill and, much to Brian's disgust, I called it a day.

I returned our skis and boots the following morning and hired snowshoes. Brian was far from impressed and complained to anyone who'd listen that I was ruining his holiday. The gods looked down kindly on me, though, and blizzard conditions set in for the next day. We are bluebird skiers – neither of us wants to ski without visibility.

~·~

By the end of 2013, we knew that travelling had become too hard for Brian to manage. Flights and hotels had become frightening for him, and even escalators and moving walkways were impossible for him to use. I could not hold his hand, carry our luggage and navigate airports at the same time. We had a few long weekends away with friends but being away from home, long car trips, public toilets and restaurants caused Brian to be fearful and for me to be so stressed that none of these things continued to be fun.

But I wanted life to be normal. I kept organising normal things and expecting normal outcomes.

After a little consultation with our two sons, we booked a week in Port Douglas in mid-2013. Brian and I had taken Liam to North Queensland some years before and had a fabulous day on the barrier reef snorkelling from a boat, cruising the river to see crocodiles and looking for cassowaries in the Daintree. The boys were young men now but I just wanted a bit of that old family togetherness that I remembered from when they were children. Brett's girlfriend, Lucy, would come too – she had never been to Queensland.

Poor Brian probably just wanted a quiet time in familiar surroundings with his usual routine. I was promising everyone a beautiful family holiday. I was sure I could deliver it. As it turns out, I was delusional. It was my fantasy, not theirs.

I booked two apartments in the centre of town, side by side, each with a spa bath and access to the pool from the balconies. I had visions of us all sitting quietly on the beach or by the pool, sipping cocktails and laughing together, having dinners in nice restaurants. It would be like holidays in the past, only better because now my children were adults and we could all go away as friends.

Our first challenge was the airport. Liam found it difficult seeing how much attention Brian needed, and he felt that everyone was looking at us. Already at least two of us were upset, and a security officer came over to check that all was okay.

When we arrived in Cairns, I dragged everyone around the supermarket to buy groceries; I had thought that eating breakfast in one of the apartments together would be a nice start to each day and save some money. If we ate lunch in or packed picnics, I thought, then I could take us all out for dinner each evening.

As with any shopping excursion, Brian became agitated and impatient. I reacted grumpily and started ordering everyone around, forgetting that they were all adults.

We drove to Port Douglas and arrived early evening. I put all the groceries in our room and established that breakfast would be a family event in the morning. Later, we could hear the young ones drinking and laughing in their spa bath. Brian could not negotiate the steps of our spa bath. He went to sleep early.

In the morning, I set the table for five and waited. At about 10 am Brett called in to pick up a box of cereal and some milk.

I tried to get Brian into the pool – we had a ladder from our 'swim out' balcony. He could not manage it, so I walked him outside to use the wide steps into the pool. The pool was clear and clean, and met all the safety requirements for hotel pools. But Brian could not perceive the pool depth or see the stairs, so he was too frightened to get in. His eyesight had not necessarily deteriorated but the messages his eyes sent to his brain were not being properly received. He was hot, so we returned to the air con in the room.

In fact, most of our time was spent in our apartment, or driving around in the air-conditioned rental car while Brian slept. We did have a lovely trip to an animal park together, and a fabulous night at a pub for dinner and a trivia competition. I drove into the

Daintree one afternoon, with Brett and Lucy. Brian napped in the car as we drove and looked at the surroundings from the window. We stopped at a roadside bar but waking him to go inside made him upset and disorientated, so we turned around and headed back to Port Douglas.

It was stinger season, so the beach was out for swimming and Brian was convinced that even walking on the beach put us in danger of a crocodile attack. On a couple of afternoons, Brett helped me get Brian into the pool and he enjoyed it while he felt safe, but his agitation quickly returned each time.

I don't know how I even imagined that Brian's problems might disappear for a week's holiday. Being in an unfamiliar environment seemed to exacerbate his agitation. It was hard work and essentially disappointing for me.

I hoped to create memories of one last family holiday full of joy and happiness, but I had become so caught up in what I wanted from the trip that I had forgotten that Brett and Liam were going through the same grief as I was. They wanted happy parents who were on the sidelines of their lives, listening to the stories of *their* new experiences in the world. They too wanted to feel the joy of previous holidays and to forget what real life was throwing at them now.

At home, they were a little removed from their dad's new needs, and I had tried to protect them from some of his more peculiar behaviours. Being thrown into 24-hour contact with him for seven days must have been a shock. The whole trip, starting at the airport, was confronting for them. I wanted them to help care for Brian but of course they did not yet have any real experience of that.

I had lost my strong, sensible, clever, loving husband and best friend. They had lost their strong, sensible, clever, loving dad and best friend.

Ah … hindsight.

Dear Brett, Liam and Lucy,

I really do hope your holiday was fun. I know you said it was, but I couldn't tell if you were just being polite.

I had hoped that we would spend a little more time together than we did, but I also wanted you guys to have a good time. The holiday was meant to be our gift to all of you – one last holiday before you were completely grown up and living your own lives.

In my dreams, I wanted it to be just like our last trip to Disneyland in 2005. Happy, funny, relaxing togetherness. I did not anticipate the pressure I would feel or the pressure I would put you under.

It was the loneliest time I have ever spent with my family.

SIX

Adjustments

The biggest impact on our lives was the change the disease caused in our family. As Brian became more dependent on me, I became more like his mother than his wife, and our boys felt the loss of their dad. The close relationship they had with him as they were growing up died, and their sadness was – and still is – very evident. It is only recently that Liam can tell me stories of times he spent with his father with a smile on his face. For years after Brian died, Liam would leave the room to hide tears when his father's name was mentioned.

As a child, Liam was always at his happiest on a road trip to Canberra or at a game with his dad. At the outset of quite a few family outings, Liam would ask me, 'Can't you just sit in the back, Mum, so I can talk to Dad?' He was always self-conscious and shy, and hid behind a façade of cheekiness, but Brian seemed to understand Liam better than anyone else.

When Brett started playing in bands, Brian watched all of them (good and bad) perform in local halls and pubs. Brett became involved in local theatre and studied performance at university, and Brian and I never missed a performance.

Now that had all changed, and Brian needed caring for much earlier in his life than any of us could have imagined. Over time, the boys learned to help me to care for him – how to help shower, dress and feed him. They were patient and sweet to him when they were around, and they did not mind helping because they did not have to do it very often. At the end of a tiring day, if they saw me impatient with him, they could not understand where my frustration and grief came from. They wanted me to be kind and loving and patient all the time. That is what I wanted to be, too. Unfortunately, I am just human.

This was not how Brian and I had envisaged these years of parenting our boys, and watching them grow into young men, and I'm sure it was not how Brett and Liam had imagined their relationship with their father would be through these years. So many wonderful things were happening in their lives; it is a privilege for parents to share those things, and I so wanted Brian to join in his boys' achievements. I tried to get him involved even when I knew it might be too much for him. So many times, I tried to carry on as though life was as it had always been, in the hope of still capturing some joy – especially the joy we had anticipated in our babies' futures.

But trying to appear normal and adjusting the world around me to fit was exhausting. I spent a lot of time just thinking about the easiest thing to do and hoping I could do it. I knew, though, that if I wanted a normal, happy life, I had to consider everyone.

And often the extra effort was worth it!

In 2013, Brett and Lucy were graduating together from the University of Wollongong. When Lucy's dad, Tim, called to say they wanted to take them out for dinner after their graduation ceremony, I did not know what to do. I wanted to celebrate the occasion too, but I had been thinking of a quiet family meal at home, maybe with Brett's favourite dishes. It was wrong of me to forget that Brett and Lucy were partners, but I was selfishly looking to have our boy to ourselves.

I told Tim that we could not really do restaurants anymore and that Brian would be happier at home. After a bit of consultation, we agreed that Lucy's family, our family and two sets of grandparents would come for dinner. Twelve people!

I started to have an anxiety attack. How would I tidy up enough, shop for the meal, prepare the meal, mow the lawn, get ready, dress Brian, get to the uni on time, serve the meal, clean up, and stay sane and calm?

Guess what? I did it!

The days beforehand were very boring for Brian, but he was patient while I got the house ready, the shopping done and the meal prepared. It was tough on him to sit for so long during the graduation ceremony but, except for a little anxiety towards the end, he did really well. I was just as proud of how well he coped as I was of Brett receiving his degree with distinction.

I would have loved for Brian to be able to see Brett get his degree. He was in the hall with me but from where we sat, all the formalities were completely out of his focus. I know he couldn't follow the ceremony. But I also know that he understood how much Brett wanted him there.

Now, when I look back on that day, all the unimportant, stressful details are gone from my memory. I do, however, remember sitting proudly in the hall at the University of Wollongong. I remember laughing and having photographs taken. I remember watching Brett and his friends and their jubilation. I don't remember what we ate for dinner, but I recall sitting in our backyard, celebrating the end of an era and two young people eager to start the next phase of their lives.

At other times, it was the simple, quiet moments at home that meant the most. Brett moved to Sydney not long after his graduation, and when he visited it was a joy for Brian and I to sit together for a family meal and to listen to what he was doing in his theatre career. Brett was well aware of how important 'normal' family evenings were, and he worked hard to make it appear effortless to spend time with us, just to make his dad smile.

I was, and still am, so grateful to the boys for all they did.

Dear Brett and Liam,

Tonight we spent one of those rare family nights in.

    I nagged you two a little about drinking and smoking (but that's my job).

    You make Dad and I so happy when we watch you sitting together and laughing together.

    You both sat with Dad and listened when he tried to tell you something without using nouns or verbs.

    Thank you, my beautiful boys.

    We love you both so much.

SEVEN

The complications of intimacy

Once Brian had 'confessed' his symptoms to his work colleagues, friends and family, he started to see the value in the YOD support group. He began to realise that organisations dedicated to the care of people suffering from dementia were an important source of up-to-date information on treatments and research, and he soon became determined to beat the disease. So he joined me at support group meetings and made new, very important friends with fellow sufferers and professionals alike.

We attended all the seminars on younger onset dementia that were offered to us. We went to conferences in Sydney and Wollongong. When Brian could no longer attend, I went on my own, when respite was available. I found the speakers validating, especially the ones with experiences similar to mine.

I cried when I listened to the children of sufferers talk about losing their parent; I empathised when I heard partners talk of caring out of love; and I listened intently when psychologists talked about cognitive therapies and adjusting our lives to manage the needs of both parties.

Our support group also discussed sex.

One of our closest friends, who cared for his wife, was concerned that he might one day be accused of sexual assault and wanted to know where that line might be drawn. He still shared a bed with his wife, and she sometimes woke in the night frightened because she did not recognise him. She did not want to sleep alone in another room, but things changed for her during the night: she would know him when they retired to bed but at 2 am, when she needed to be taken to the bathroom, she expected the husband she remembered aged 25 to be beside her – not the same man 30 years of lost memory later. He was frightened that consensual sex could change during the act. Then what? He worried a little about his safety, but he worried mostly about her feelings and fears.

But in all the advice given to us by professionals, the subjects that everyone studiously avoided were intimacy and sex.

Psychologists, doctors, social workers and care workers all talked about how Brian would lose his planning abilities, his motor skills, his verbal skills and his sight recognition. I learned strategies to compensate for these losses. But none of them told me what I should do when he stops giving me a cuddle, telling me I look nice, climbing into the shower with me to wash my back, bringing home flowers for no reason, making me a cup of tea after dinner or waking me with one in the morning, and – most importantly – reaching across to stroke me softly when he wants to make love.

I don't know what I wanted from a professional that I did not know how to try myself. I could show Brian physical comfort. I could still touch him and get a response; sometimes that response was just that he would relax and go to sleep.

I wanted all the things that were never going to happen again.

Brian and I had tried hard for our whole marriage to keep our love life special and romantic. There were no grand gestures, just regular loving gestures. I remember when we moved into our first home, we made love in every room! We always held hands when walking together, sat close on the couch to watch TV, and slept touching so the space between us was never too big. We talked every day if one of us was away from home. We said 'I love you' every day and meant it. We kissed and nuzzled and stroked like teenagers. It made our children cringe! We tried hard to keep sex intimate and romantic and spontaneous.

When Brian was first diagnosed, our sex life and our libidos suffered, until we realised that our time together was going to be shorter than we had planned. Then we decided to live our lives to the full, to take joy where we found it and to magnify it if we could.

So our love life flourished again. We took holidays – and holiday sex is always good! We revelled in what we could still do. We swam on tropical reefs, skied down mountains, walked in the Swiss Alps, cruised, drove, hiked. And we made love like we had in our twenties.

In those early stages, I pushed hard to keep intimacy alive. I took the upper hand, became the romantic one, instigated sex, planned romantic dates – roles we had previously shared. Brian's doctors were astounded to hear we were still intimate, despite him taking risperidone. One of the side effects of this anti-psychotic medication was supposed to be impotency. What can I say? He was a fit and determined man!

We hid from the inevitable, but it tracked us down. I noticed the changes, but Brian did not. I didn't point them out to him. I grieved for our connection alone.

As time wore on, he did not see my hints. He went to sleep while I tickled his back, became frustrated if meals were served too slowly in restaurants, did not want to hold hands if we went for a walk because I walked slower than him, hated watching a movie because he could not follow the plot. He couldn't sit with me in the evening – or anytime – because he would pace through the house. If it was dark, he thought it was bedtime. He would climb into bed still dressed and be asleep before I could help him get undressed. He hated showers and teeth cleaning. He needed help to dress, to eat, to go to the toilet.

I needed to give him step-by-step instructions on how to do all the little things in life. Those instructions became a constant nagging in his ears. Listening to me and being frustrated by not being able to do things just left him angry.

For me, the loss of these parts of our marriage has been the cause of some of the greatest pain in this journey.

Dear Brian,

Who the hell could I write this to except you? When do I ever discuss the intimacy in our marriage with anyone other than you?

Having you so near me yet so removed from me is the saddest part of this journey. You have been my husband for 36 years, my lover for more than 40 years, and now I don't have that part of you anymore.

I miss holding your hand because it means togetherness, not because I need to restrain you so you do not trip into traffic.

I miss having my back washed in the shower. Being woken by a hand stroking my arm.

I miss you creeping up behind me and kissing my neck while I cook dinner.

I miss being on the pedestal you put me on.

I miss being touched with affection.

I miss being needed. I miss being loved.

EIGHT

Teamwork

The St George Illawarra rugby league club has a first-grade reunion event every year. Brian's 1979 team, perhaps because they were grand final winners, always attend, and it is rare for one of them to miss it.

Brian loved going to the reunion each year, but when we received the invitation for the 2014 reunion, I wasn't sure if he would be able to manage a night like that. The event is always held in the function room above the grandstand at Kogarah Oval. It is exclusively for men that have played first grade for the Dragons and it is a tradition that I know goes back a long way – my grandfather used to attend in the 1950s and '60s. It involves eating and drinking and reminiscing for a full afternoon. The men I know who attend always need to be collected at the end, as none of them can ever drive home.

Then one of Brian's closest mates from that era, John Jansen, called to let me know about the reunion – and to make sure I knew that he and Brian's former teammates would look after him on the night. John lives in Wollongong, close enough to visit Brian fairly regularly. By seeing us more often than most, he was aware of some of our struggles, and his consideration was wonderful.

John's thoughtfulness made a big difference to us, and Brian was delighted when I told him he would be going to the reunion with his friends.

I learned the great value of being part of a team when Brian became ill. My dad was a wonderful father but he had some very fixed ideas on sport, including that it was for men and boys, not girls. Girls were not supposed to have muscles – they were supposed to cook and sew. The upshot of that attitude was that I never experienced playing a team sport.

Brian built wonderful relationships in his teams, friendships that really did last to the end of his life. Teammates from his high school and junior league days at Dapto, through to his 1979 grand final–winning team at St George, his colleagues from his coaching and administrative roles, and the wonderful rugby league organisation Men of League all gave him – and me – unwavering support. They still do.

The men from the team of 1979 are close and I can only speculate that they discussed between themselves how they would help Brian on the day. They effortlessly took over the role of carer from me and I had nothing but confidence when I left him with them. I know how highly he regarded them. I suspect they loved him too.

Rugby league players often get bad press about their attitudes to women and their poor role modelling. In my experience, these big, tough men are gentle and caring. On many occasions, Brian was included in outings where he needed assistance to negotiate steps to get into a bus, help to eat a meal and to even be assisted in the toilet.

I watched some of these big, tough men try to hide tears as they included him in their events and make sure he had fun. No one ever told me it was too hard to take him. When I would suggest he would be too much trouble for them, they insisted on taking him with them.

I know these dinners and get-togethers were the highlights in his life in his last couple of years.

Brian is not the only person these men have cared for. Old(er) rugby league players are wonderful friends. I am so glad to have had them in our lives.

Dear 'Boys',

That seems a silly thing to write but I am not sure what to call you collectively. 'Team of '79' doesn't seem right, and I don't want your title to be too long and explanatory. I don't mean just the team players, either: club directors, training staff from when Brian played, and staff he worked with in later years – you are all in this!

Today was the St George first-grade reunion. Brian's invitation arrived about four weeks ago. I should really learn not to tell him anything too early. He has been getting cross with me almost every evening since because I haven't taken him to the reunion. I have tried to explain that I cannot get him there until the actual day, but he has just felt like he has waited too long to go. I need to give him things to look forward to, and I need to talk to him too – when the invitation arrived it gave me something to tell him, and to try to have a conversation about. But it was at the cost of his impatience and anger.

Anyway, today was the day and he was excited to be going – like a child to a birthday party! He grinned almost all the way there in the car, though was pretty agitated when I hit a little traffic on the trip. But when he saw the grandstand, his anger dissipated and he was the grinning child again as we walked into the venue.

As usual, there were some men in the grounds stopping players for autographs on their memorabilia. I was dreading it, as they had stopped us and made a request last year, and I'd had to explain that Brian could no longer write. This year, they acknowledged us but did not ask Brian to sign anything.

I thought it was very respectful that they remembered what I had told them last year.

We walked up the stairs and were embraced by Steve Edge, the 1979 team captain, who got Brian a drink and took over my role of carer.

I knew Brian would have a wonderful time and that he would be well taken care of. When John Jansen brought him back to me, where I had waited with other wives across the road at St George Leagues Club, Brian couldn't really tell me what he'd done or who he'd seen but his happiness was written all over his face.

I wish I had played a team sport. Even now, 35 years on, you guys are such good friends. He loves you all. He is so comfortable with all of you, and he trusts you all implicitly. I would love to have a support group like that!

Thanks for today, guys. For as long as he can remember he was there, he will grin every time I mention it. It will bring him joy for weeks.

NINE

Friends who give

I have heard some people say that they have felt abandoned by family and friends after a dementia diagnosis. I never experienced that. I felt lonely at times, but that was not because people walked away from us.

Perhaps it is also a reflection of what we had invested in our friends prior to the diagnosis. Everyone's situation is different.

Since our return from England, we had made a point of visiting Les and Judy Boyd about four times a year. The trip had always involved a golfing day between the fiercely competitive Les and the even more competitive Brian. Staying with our good friends was something we both always looked forward to.

At the Boyds' invitation, we drove to Cootamundra for a New Year's Eve barbecue in 2013. They were having friends over for a night by their pool and Brian was very excited by the prospect of joining them. We planned to stay for two nights.

On the way, the four-hour drive extended out to six and a half hours as Brian became agitated in the car and we stopped a little more often than usual. It was a more stressful trip than I had anticipated, and I was pleased and relieved to arrive safely. Brian had been so excited at the prospect of seeing our friends and he was familiar with their house, so I thought he would settle down once we arrived.

But as soon as we had said our hellos to the Boyds, Brian wanted me to take him home. I had to explain to him that I could not just turn around and drive all the way back to Wollongong – I was too tired.

Les and his mates managed to distract Brian for a while, but his agitation did not leave him. As usual, it manifested in restlessness. It almost looked like he was trying to find an escape route from the garden, which was fenced on all sides.

We left to return home at 8 am the following morning, after a sleepless night that had nothing to do with the noise of the New Year celebrations.

During that long evening, though, even the guests who we did not already know took turns at walking with Brian as he paced around the yard, and trying to engage him in conversation. Sometimes these efforts put in by people we did not expect help from – let alone the generosity of our friends – brightened our lives and gave us the joy we had planned to find in our remaining days together.

Outside of our new dementia support-group friends, our social circle altered a little when our closest friend's marriage broke up. We lost some friends – and we gained some. His new partner became part of our lives, and her family and friends welcomed us in.

To this day, these wonderful people are still my friends. I barely knew them when I wrote this letter. I am so lucky to have them in my life!

Dear Jenny, Jan, Al, John, Annette, Cath, Brian, Wendy, Mary, Steve, Jez, Cat, Tim and Ben,

We spent an evening with you all tonight and we had such a good time.

None of you knew Brian before he had dementia. Some of you met him in the early stages of the disease and just thought him a little ditzy. Some of you met him after many of his physical symptoms had kicked in.

All of you treat him like an old friend. All of you treat him with such respect! You make allowances for him, but you do it so well he barely notices.

You engage him in conversation. You feed him dip and hold his drink for him. You calm him down.

You are a wonderful group of people and I thank you all very much for your friendship.

I wish you could have known him before.

TEN

On the road

Brian had always liked to drive, but driving became one of the biggest dangers in our lives – for both of us.

One of Brian's great pleasures in life was driving interesting roads, especially on our travels. The cars travel very fast on motorways in Europe, and Brian would always drive at a safe speed in the slow lane while I read a book or napped in my seat. His diaries from our holidays in Europe document the mountain passes and gorges we drove through in France, Italy, Norway and Switzerland. I can remember feeling carsick as we wound our way along the edge of cliffs and climbed steep peaks on gravel roads to get the best vantage points for his photographs – even in howling winds that had me sure we would be blown off.

Before his diagnosis, Brian started to become a nervous passenger. On a week away skiing with friends in 2009, Garry drove them along Guthega Road between Jindabyne and Perisher, a lovely winding road that follows a ridge above the Snowy River. It is not particularly high or frightening but Brian became quite agitated, and Garry decided to turn around as requested so as not to upset him further. No one else was scared; they thought Brian was just unused to travelling by road in the snow (he usually took the ski tube to begin his day). Before any of us were aware of a problem,

Brian's brain was already letting him down and taking away his joy.

One night, before his diagnosis, he rang me while driving home from Sydney. He was coming down the Bulli Pass, a steep mountain road that runs from the top of the Illawarra escarpment to the coast. It has high banks on both sides of the road as it winds with the natural contours of the mountain, and is known locally as a dangerous road – for good reason.

Brian was driving his automatic Commodore station wagon. 'There's something wrong with the car,' he told me over the phone. 'I put it into second, and it went into reverse!' The mechanic could not duplicate that problem the next day, but Brian insisted that he had put the car into second gear, not reverse, while driving at 60 kilometres an hour down Bulli Pass.

Although he did not agree that his driving skills were diminishing, he did eventually give up his licence voluntarily. After his diagnosis, he knew that insurance would not cover him if he had an accident. I persuaded him that without insurance we might lose the house if we had to pay someone else's medical costs.

I wanted to sell his car. I was frightened that he would find the key, which I had hidden, and drive somewhere when I was at work, despite no longer having a licence. He was actually too much of a rule-follower to do that, but forgetting that he no longer had a licence was a real possibility.

He insisted we still needed a station wagon, so we sold his car and traded mine in for a car that was much bigger and more expensive than we required. He was a bit happier, though, having contributed to the decision himself.

As his dementia progressed, the car became a frighteningly small space for him, and he felt locked in. He would forget how to use a door handle and try to exit the car by opening the glovebox. This may sound funny, but the frustration and anger he felt when he was 'trapped' in the car was anything but funny. I was lucky to have a friendly mechanic who understood our situation, and he disconnected the cable on the inside front door handle. It was an unsafe thing to do, as a passenger could not get out of the car by themselves in an accident, but that risk was far outweighed by the risk of Brian falling from an open door onto a busy road.

The letter here documents just one of the small incidents I had while distracted by Brian in the car. Luckily the others all involved gutters and not pedestrians.

Dear Brian,

Bugger!

Today I pulled into a disabled parking space and left you in the car with your good mate Thommo, who had come along for the ride, while I ran into the office to pick up some paperwork.

When I came out, you were trying to get out of the car, and I was running late to get you to the doctor. I paid too much attention to you and turned the car into the bright-yellow metal bollard to my right. Knocked it right out of the ground and ran over it, and made a big mess of the front of the car.

It could have been *so* much worse.

Just last week I had the door handle on the car disconnected after you opened it while I was doing 80 kilometres an hour on Lake Entrance Road. It was so lucky there wasn't a car in the other lane, or that you hadn't undone your seatbelt as well.

Car trips over the past few weeks have been a nightmare. I cannot work out if it is the confined space of the car, if you are uncomfortable, or if you are just plain scared of being driven anywhere.

I am so glad I only hit a bollard, and not a pedestrian or another car.

Guess we'll be staying home a lot more!

ELEVEN

A man of words

Brian was always a 'man of few words' – the yin to my yang (I am a trifle verbose at times!). But he was clever with language, and a good teacher who could explain what he wanted clearly and concisely. And he was a voracious reader with a great vocabulary who wrote poems – long ballads – to his friends on special occasions.

His university friends recall how little time he would need to study before exams. On days they had set aside to swot so that they could imprint the names of muscles and bones on their brains ahead of an anatomy and physiology exam, Brian would arrive two hours later with his golf clubs, asking why they hadn't finished memorising. He would have created a string of silly phrases to remember the relevant information, like 'pissing triangles in the loo gives you scaphoid' (pisiform triquetrum lunate scaphoid) for the bones in the wrist. His memory for facts and details was amazing and he almost always achieved distinctions on his papers.

He was an asset to any trivia team we ever played on, recalling facts on sport, history and science, and never needing time to recall an answer. In the heyday of trivia nights as fundraisers, we would regularly attend with friends and often take out first prize. Never a million dollars – usually a voucher for $50 or so to be divided among a team of eight. So, for Brian, losing his abilities with language was horrible.

Language dyspraxia is the inability to form words properly. Aphasia is the inability to find the words you want to say. Brian developed both symptoms.

He often knew what he wanted to say but could not find the words to express his thoughts. He seemed to lose the ability to use nouns or verbs.

He would begin a sentence and look at me. In the early stages of his dementia, it was often a stop in conversation where he would appear to have just lost his train of thought and many times, in context, I knew what he wanted to tell me. If he was speaking to someone else, there was a good chance I could finish the sentence for him.

As the dementia got worse, he would begin a sentence without any context at all and look at me to finish it for him. It was obvious that he knew what he wanted to say. His frustration at me for not helping properly was apparent. His anger at me for what he presumed I was doing on purpose to belittle him was something I did not expect, and it was frightening at times.

Dear Brian,

Dear God! (I mean that in the profane way.) I cannot understand half of the things you say to me now. You mumble words and then look quizzical – as if it was me who said them. Your sentences start but don't finish, and you get really cross with me when I don't know what you are trying to tell or ask me.

'What was the name of ... you know him ... we talked about him before ...'

'Do you remember when ... you know we did ... can't you remember?'

'What are we going to do on … ?'

'I don't want to … I told you before … I tell you all the time …'

'Have a look at yourself …'

'Are you *drunk*?'

'Where is my friend … you know … you won't let me see him …'

I am so sorry.

I try repeating the beginning of your sentence back to you; I try guessing; I tell you I am listening; I wait for ages. I feel like my brain is swelling inside my head as I try to work out what you mean. You stare at me with such anger. Sometimes I think you are going to hit me you look so cross.

I wish I could solve these conundrums. I want to help you. I want to talk to you. I want to communicate with words.

We still do communicate sometimes with a smile or a touch. I know what that means. I know when that happens, you are happy, that you love me. But I want to talk about *stuff*: about the boys, the past, the future. I want to ask your advice – it was always so sound and sensible. I hate making all the decisions.

I miss you so much, my darling. Please come back.

TWELVE

How not to help

Sometimes families fall out. Brian and I both come from happy, close families. We were lucky enough to have had parents who were happily married – great role models for both of us. We have three siblings each, all of whom have lovely partners and children. The Johnson and Robinson families would have the usual get-togethers at birthdays, christenings, weddings and Christmases. Those events were important to Brian and to me.

Over the years, a small matter became a bigger one and some cross words were exchanged between Brian and one family member. Brian was a remarkably forgiving person, and if it hadn't been for his dementia I know this problem would have been overcome and forgotten about in the ensuing years. However, at the time I wrote this letter in 2013, it was raw and the quarrel was relatively fresh.

This letter was written in anger, but it is anger I have not held on to. It is the one letter I did post. I do not regret sending it, as it was very important to me at the time and needed to be said. Here I have included it, in an edited form, because it comprehensively outlines the symptoms that Brian suffered at the time, and I wanted this family member to truly understand what Brian was going through.

Dear _____,

I challenge you to read this letter to the end. I would come to talk to you but anticipate that it would be futile. I write just so you understand what has happened to Brian.

I write this with a mix of sadness and anger.

Sadness that a family is broken.

Anger that you broke it.

There is no way that the local grapevine did not inform you at least two years ago of Brian's illness.

We have never heard a word from you or your immediate family to enquire about his health.

I did not really care until I heard comments relayed from one of your children recently. He'd said that Brian did not speak when he saw him, and that it was because Brian thought your son was you and he is not speaking to you.

Brian has not forgotten anyone.

He has never stopped speaking to you, and he does not mistake a young man of 25 for a 60-year-old man.

But he has lost the ability to scan a room, so unless your son came and spoke directly to him, Brian simply would not have seen him. His focus is on his immediate surroundings and his companion.

If you take some sort of comfort in thinking that you don't need to see him because he doesn't know you anymore, then you are very wrong.

Your family – and I assume by your influence and opinions – have always been disrespectful to our family. Our children were told on many occasions that they were 'not really Johnsons'. Our boys are just as much Johnsons as I am. The processes of marriage and adoption have the same outcomes.

Sadly, you have always placed your children in a position of competition against their cousins. Families should not be in competition. Families are there to give love to each other.

I have not seen you display love to anyone in all the years I have known you.

I want you to understand what has happened to Brian.

Brian was diagnosed just three years ago with younger onset dementia, Alzheimer's type, and I suspect he has had the symptoms of this disease for about six years.

He began to have tests to find why he felt he was living in a fog, could not retain the words he was studying in his master's degree, and kept forgetting the names of player moves he had devised. He did not take one day off work.

He first saw a neurologist in June 2010, and his final diagnosis was in August. We were in shock.

Brian has lost many abilities. First were his abilities to plan and problem solve. He ceased to drive. He found it harder and harder to see things directly in front of him. His balance suffered. He developed myoclonic jerks in his left arm. His peripheral vision declined. He could not hold a train of thought in conversation. He stopped being able to use the computer, his mobile phone, the television, keys, door handles, books, coat hangers, cutlery, taps, the washing machine, pegs, garden tools, shoelaces … the list goes on. He cannot sustain an interest long enough to watch a movie or a game of rugby league.

His long-term memory hasn't been affected yet and he remembers everyone although he may struggle to use their name. His short-term memory is very affected – he cannot hold plans in his head and has trouble with timing of upcoming events.

I cut my work back to three days a week in 2011 but retired from work in August this year to care for him full-time.

Currently Brian has severe dyspraxia and language dyspraxia. He knows what he wants to say but cannot locate the word he needs. He cannot dress himself. He cannot feed himself unless he uses his fingers and even that is difficult. He needs help to shower. He cannot shave. He needs assistance to go to the toilet. He needs assistance to sit on a chair.

Sometimes he cannot work out how to lie down in bed. He occasionally displays psychosis but has it under control with mild medication and his usual sense of right and wrong. He walks constantly in the house – like a lion pacing in a cage. At times he is effectively blind, because the messages sent from his eyes to his brain do not always work. He no longer reads or writes. He visits his mother at least three times a week – she is unaware of his problems and he 'hides' from her, keeping their conversation light and relying on me to answer her questions.

He smiles, he laughs, and he loves me and his boys. He is immensely proud of both of them. He loves music. He loves to dance with me. His dancing is still terrible. He is sad for what he has lost and is losing still. He knows he is dying.

He is the bravest person I have ever met.

He cries occasionally but usually due to frustration. He never feels sorry for himself. He worries constantly about me and still tries to look after me as he always has.

I ask nothing of you. I just want you to understand what is happening and have enough information about Brian so that you can answer people if you are asked how he is. Most people would not be able to comprehend that immediate family could have turned their back on one of their own.

This may not be the easiest letter for you to read. You probably don't agree with my point of view on some things. You don't have to. I merely want you to understand the truth about Brian and have your family stop filling in the gaps with assumptions.

Well done if you made it all the way through this. That is something I can respect.

THIRTEEN

Shared history

Sometimes I just wanted to talk to Brian about the minutiae of normal life. I think this still feels like my biggest loss – the simple sharing in a partnership. The understanding of little things that mean something in our family but nothing to anyone from outside it. A little shared history.

Getting together at the ages of 15 and 17 meant that so much of what we knew we had learned together. This seems to have aligned our senses of humour. We were both tragic *Fawlty Towers* and *Blackadder* fans and both hated Chevy Chase movies. We were guilty of judgementally watching people and finding the same things secretly funny at times.

Brian loved to tease those closest to him – me, Narelle, his mum. Never with any malice. He would make light of little problems to make us laugh.

When it came time to sell his parents' home and divide up their remaining possessions, that big job was shouldered by his sisters, Debbie and Narelle. I know it would have been much easier with him there to take some of the load of the decisions they had to make.

But there was one particular revelation during that process that I know we would have discussed and laughed about.

Dear Brian,

Tonight we met with your sisters, Debbie and Narelle, to take mementos from your mum's house.

There was nothing of any real value in the knick-knacks that were to be broken up, just things that your parents held dear – souvenirs from their travels, crockery given to them as wedding gifts that had never been used because it was 'too good', 1930s fine china cups and plates from your grandparents' houses, and photographs.

We divided up some china, and found your christening cup, baby photos and a toby jug I had sent your mum from England.

I wanted you to have something to help you remember your childhood home and your mum and dad. I chose the picture of autumnal trees that had been a wedding present to them and always hung on the wall in the kitchen. Your dad told me the story of how their good friends had given it to them as a wedding gift, and he and your mum had been sorely disappointed – they had thought it was a page cut out from a calendar and framed. Then one day, your dad had a good look at it and realised it was a beautiful oil painting and moved it from its hidey hole in a cupboard and displayed it proudly on the wall in the kitchen.

He must have told me that story very early on in our relationship – it feels like I have always known it. He was so very proud to own an original oil painting.

I thought that if I hung it on our kitchen wall, you could see it every day. We could have it reframed with a nice surround to set it off.

Brett studied it closely. He pried the backing from the frame and slipped the painting out.

Guess what? It's not a painting. It is a print on very flimsy paper.

We put it back in its original frame, and it now takes pride of place on the wall in our kitchen. I don't think there is any need to change the frame. It is exactly as you remember it from home.

It made us all laugh!

You would have laughed too. And you would have mercilessly teased your dad about it!

FOURTEEN

A less social life

On a winter night in 2014, Brian and I had our last dinner out with friends. It was a meal in an Asian restaurant with about five other couples. In consideration of Brian, a banquet had been ordered that consisted of quite a lot of entrees, all able to be eaten without cutlery and without attracting the attention of other restaurant patrons.

The changes in Brian happened so quickly that it was difficult to adjust. By then, Brian's ability to see the things right in front of him had declined. He would see the food on the other side of the table more easily as he looked across at companions at a table. This meant he did not eat his own meal; instead, he reached across to take the food from someone else's plate. Each friend's instinct was to give their meal to Brian and get something else, but by putting their meal in front of him it became invisible to him, and he would then pick off their new plate, starting the cycle all over again.

That night, he had decided he had enough of being inside and absconded from the restaurant when I was chatting to someone else. I spent almost all the mealtime chasing him up the highway. Brian, thinking that he was in trouble, had decided to run home. We were 30 kilometres from home and he could run much faster than I could. By the time I had found him, got him into the car and back to the restaurant I was in tears, he was cranky with me, and the meal was over.

A few weeks later, we were due to see a concert locally that included Glenn Shorrock and Brian Cadd, musicians who we both enjoyed. Brian particularly liked to see musicians that we had both listened to in our teens and twenties. Over the years we had been in audiences for some big names, including Simon and Garfunkel, Neil Diamond, Don McLean, Jackson Browne, Leonard Cohen, Bob Dylan and Boz Scaggs. Listening to them again at home and discussing those concerts together was a big part of our life now.

We'd bought the tickets a few months before the show. A lot can change in a few months.

The group of friends we were going with were meeting for dinner prior to the show and we were booked into the restaurant with them. Closer to the day, I decided a crowded restaurant would be too much for Brian, so I pulled out of the pre-show catch-up and arranged for us to meet in the foyer before the show.

We met by the door to our seating area. Anita's Theatre is a lovely concert hall in Thirroul, an old picture theatre from the 1920s restored beautifully and popular now as a live music venue. It has a winding staircase at the front entrance to get into the theatre, but the back of the building opens straight onto the street behind it, with no stairs to negotiate. It also has a bar.

The show was a sellout, but getting into our seats wasn't too bad with the assistance of our friends. I had made sure Brian had dinner at home earlier, and had not drunk too much water so he would not need the toilet during the show. I swapped tickets with a friend and Brian and I sat on the end seats of the row, just in case we had to get out in a hurry.

The show was great. Brian tapped along, sang along with the performers at times and enjoyed it immensely. He was in such a great mood that I accepted an offer to join the rest of the group at the pub across the road for a drink before we drove home.

As the lights came on, I asked him to stay in his seat so we could let the crowd disperse before we exited. All our friends were happy to wait too.

Brian watched the people in front of us stand up. He stood up. He watched people walk down the aisle. He followed them.

I had no hope of restraining him, so I just had to hold onto his arm and go with him. I thought that once we hit the foyer I would be back in control, but the crowd turned towards the stairs en masse and we were carried along with them. Stairs had become very difficult for Brian; he would hold both hands onto the balustrade and go downstairs sideways, or just stop walking altogether. That was not going to be good in this crowd.

I was trying very hard to drag Brian away from the stairs. People just saw a mad woman pushing against the flow of traffic and a cranky man trying to break away from her grip.

From nowhere, a security guard grabbed Brian and looked at me angrily, asking, 'How the hell did he become so intoxicated?'

I retorted just as angrily: 'He is not intoxicated, he is *disabled*!'

To this young man's credit, his demeanour changed immediately. He was suddenly my knight in shining armour. I told him that Brian would fall down the stairs and that I just wanted to get him to the back entrance. Brian was unbelievably rude and angry to me but, as usual, too polite to be rude to the bouncer. He acquiesced and allowed the man to steer him out of the crowd and to the back door.

His politeness evaporated as the bouncer left our side. Brian was furious with me for 'making him look like an idiot'. I was furious with him for not following my instructions and plans and for creating a scene. We glowered at each other. Our friends waited patiently outside. I asked for help to get him into the car and changed my mind about a nightcap in the pub.

Brian and I fought all the way home – me promising emphatically that we were never going out in the evenings again, him telling me that I always ruined everything for him and would not let him be with his friends anymore.

I am sure he had forgotten the concert altogether by then. He probably forgot what had made him so angry too. But the feelings of anger and disappointment stayed with him, and he had a dreadful, sleepless night.

My darling Brian,

My lost darling Brian. I am grieving for you. Where have you gone? Why can't I find you in my head and my heart anymore?

I hate the way this disease has altered the person that you were. What I hate even more is that I am so involved with your needs now that I feel like I am forgetting the person that you were. I try to think of a happy memory when these attacks happen so that I can find the tolerance to help you through them, but the here and now takes over all my memories and I cannot find the real you anymore.

I don't want to forget what we had. I want to be able to look at you and see my clever, strong, rational, kind, supportive husband. But I am overwhelmed, and I see you as a scared, irrational man-child. I am scared that I will stop loving you.

You are overshadowed by the man who looks like an older version of you. He is unreasonable and unloving. He is incredibly demanding of my time but ungrateful when I give it. He is an angry bully sometimes who talks to me in half-sentences and doesn't explain what he wants. He paces constantly and complains about me to the fellow he sees in the bathroom mirror – the one who grins at him and makes him laugh. I can make him happy with food – especially ice cream – but it is short-lived. He doesn't want to do anything but is bored all the time.

Please come back, my love. He is wearing me out and turning me into a bitter old lady.

I just want you to take care of me again.

FIFTEEN

The Happiness Project, part 1

On one of Brian's more lucid days, he told me that he had only one regret in his life. He regretted not dancing with me whenever I wanted to.

Brian was always fine to get up and dance a waltz, or even a jive or a samba. He had trained in ballroom dancing at teachers' college and taught it in his PE classes over the years he was a schoolteacher.

I don't remember ever being upset that he did not want to dance. I knew it made him feel awkward. I would just dance with my girlfriends or sometimes with one of his friends if they were with us.

He asked me once, on the way home from a music festival where everyone had danced in a field by our picnics, if I 'felt' music when I heard it. Of course I answered yes. Once the music starts, I find it hard not to dance – even on my own, even sitting in a chair. Brian said he could not feel the music so did not understand how to dance unless there were specific steps.

I hope when I come to the end of my life, I only have such tiny regrets.

One of the very few nights Brian got up and danced with me stands out in my memory as an exceptionally happy night out.

It was only a short time after we were married. A group of his college friends had gathered at a restaurant. The girls all danced, and the boys got up, leaned against a wall and moved their hands. Brian joined in too – very unusual!

Looking back at happy moments like those confirmed why I continued to look after Brian, why I didn't chuck it all in and give his care over to someone else. I knew why I was looking after him, but at times I just wanted to run away from it all.

'Living in the moment' always seems to mean finding joy in your situation, but sometimes 'living in the moment' of Brian's illness meant I was lonely and miserable. So I tried to focus on our happiest moments, and find the joy I promised we would look for every day.

―――――――――

Dear Brian,

Tonight I have put you to bed and come back downstairs. This is the third time this week I have done this. We always went to bed together. It feels strange and disloyal. I worry that you feel abandoned, but I am not yet ready to sleep. I will regret it in the morning when you wake early and want me to get up. I will want to sleep then.

I am trying to concentrate on happiness. Trying to remember when we were happiest. I am sad that it is so hard to do. It is as though my memory is fading. I feel like I am losing touch with the real you and can only remember this shadow that you are now. Your condition overshadows what we used to call our 'blessed life'.

So I am reaching into my tired brain to find some of those happy memories. To pick moments of joy in our lives. There is no 'happiest moment' – there were so many. Some were huge, and some would look insignificant to anyone else.

I just remember that we were often joyous.

- The first night we spent together – I was 17 and you were 19. On the floor at your cousins' house. I was so excited I could not sleep.
- The day Dapto won the grand final in 1978. You were ecstatic and I could not stop grinning. My work colleagues thought I was silly, but it was the biggest thing in your life at the time.
- Driving the Great Ocean Road. I remember eating cream teas and looking at the beautiful views. We did not plan the trip very well – the banks were closed over a long weekend. We ran out of money and had to live on the bread and jam we had left in the esky for two days until the bank opened again. We stayed at a horrible campsite at Lakes Entrance and laughed at how silly we were.
- The day you said you wanted to get married. I couldn't believe it was really happening.
- Our wedding day.
- St George winning the 1979 grand final.
- The day you gave me the sapphire ring you had bought in Thailand. You gave me some ugly handbags and a jacket, and I was a little disappointed – all the other boys had purchased jewellery. But I knew it was not like you to spend money like that, and certainly not on jewellery. You held the ring back and gave it to me hours later. I loved it!
- Leaving for England – what an adventure! Holding hands and walking up Walton Road in Stockton Heath on our first morning there. We both couldn't stop smiling.
- Our first trip to Disneyland. We were like little children.
- The day we picked Brett up and took him home. We were besotted. If I look at the copious photos of us with him, I see nothing but joy.
- Celebrating Warrington's game at Wembley – anyone would've thought we had won.
- The wedding anniversary we spent in bed eating Chinese food from Marks & Spencer.

- The happy chaos of the day we were told we had a second son, and Liam arrived just hours later.

I need to keep adding to this list, but it has made me smile just to write what I have; so, writing it has done its job. Joyous moments came easily to me when I let myself think of them.

I owe you every happiness I have had since I was 15 years old.

I remember how you always made me feel so cared for, so loved. So happy. That's why I loved you and I love you still. I just need to remember I am your wife, not just your carer. That's why I stay your wife. Because I still love you. The real you. The one who is still there under the ugly black stuff on your brain. The one hidden from me sometimes but who surfaces for brief moments to tell me how much you love me and to thank me for being with you.

I will write more, but now I am ready to go up to bed with you.

SIXTEEN

How to care

It is hard for people who are not professionally trained, or who do not live with someone with a disability, to understand how to treat a person with cognitive decline. Everyone deserves respect.

The decline of a person's cognition can be slow or sudden. Something they could do yesterday can be gone tomorrow. Sometimes they can start something quite capably only to lose the ability to complete the task.

Caring for Brian evolved that way for me. Whenever Brian felt under pressure, his anxiety stopped him from being able to communicate as quickly as he needed to. I tried to ease this pressure by giving him the time to communicate just with me, and then I would advocate for him. I am not sure people always recognised that when I asked for something for him, it was what he wanted for himself, because he had told me. I was not always making all the decisions; I was often just his mouthpiece.

During the journey, the line between caregiver and wife began to blur. But I was always Brian's wife first, and I wanted him with me. I know he also wanted to be with me, at home where he felt safe.

Brian's former GP, Dr Jones, had become a specialist and Brian had not been under his care since 2011. So I took Brian to see the

GP that I had been seeing for years. He was a lovely and kind man, but I did not like the way he dealt with Brian. He wasn't unkind in any way, and he did not mean to be disrespectful, but he always spoke to me instead of Brian.

Because of Brian's language difficulties, if he wanted to see the doctor, I would spend the time before the appointment eliciting from Brian what he wanted to say, or where he had pain. It was often laborious and frustrating for Brian but by the time we got to our appointment I could save the doctor a lot of frustration.

I would begin the consultation by saying, 'Brian wants to know …' or 'Brian has discomfort here …'

Even though Brian would be in the room with me listening, and he would submit to any examination required, the GP only ever addressed me. I felt that Brian deserved to be treated like and spoken to as an adult. I was there to play a passive listening role and then carry out the doctor's instructions.

After one visit, the doctor walked with us into the waiting room. He put his hand on my shoulder and said, 'You don't have to do this, you know. There is no shame in putting him into a nursing home.'

I was taken aback by the comment. I wanted support from my GP for what I was doing – I did not want a way out! He was a knowledgeable and caring doctor, but he was trying to care for me, not for Brian. I wanted Brian to be just as important as he had always been.

I was lucky to find another GP in the same practice who held a master's in geriatrics. He had more experience in the field, and he instantly suited us. Brian became his patient, and the new GP showed him the respect and care he deserved. Because of his local work with geriatric patients, he knew and worked closely with Brian's geriatrician, Dr Clair Langford. That made me even more confident I had found the best GP for Brian.

We were lucky to have professional carers who were highly trained and empathetic. Our care provider was Community Options Illawarra, and there I was guided by a wonderful case manager and other staff. I am also incredibly grateful for the financial support of our welfare system, which meant I could look after Brian myself at home.

HammondCare ran a seven-day, live-in course at their Miranda facility when it first opened. It was wonderful. Brian and I had already accepted some professional assistance at home but this course was designed to teach carers strategies for assisting our partners in our day-to-day activities, and to educate us on the latest research and other options available to carers. Its main objective was to ensure that the carers did not burn out. A group of five couples were invited to participate in the inaugural program. We all stayed together in a cottage on site, and it felt like a holiday.

After breakfast each morning, our partners were taken on outings and the carers went to classes that covered everything from the legal aspects to the medical issues of dementia. We came back together each night for dinner. One evening, following a talk on reminiscence that included music, we borrowed the tapes, pushed back the tables and danced. We played cards, drank wine, and chatted and laughed together.

On the last night there, I told Brian we would be going home the next morning, and he asked if we could stay longer as it was the best holiday he had had for years.

I came away feeling prepared for anything and with a couple of wonderful new friends.

The role of community care workers in the system of aged and disability care is so important. As I see it, they undertake their roles differently not based on their training and professionalism but on their personalities. Beyond the standard training, I do not think a professional carer needs much more qualification for the job than an empathetic and compassionate attitude towards the people they are caring for. Some care workers are just in a job and they know how to follow policies and procedures. For others it is a vocation and they know how to relate to their clients. Brian and I experienced both types of professional carer, but we remembered the ones who made us feel like friends. A little training in this field cannot possibly make you good at it if your personality does not suit it.

Once I had given up work I needed a little time to myself sometimes, and Brian needed to be stimulated by the company of someone other than me. But for longer than necessary, I resisted the advice to have someone assist Brian to shower and get ready in the morning. I just felt like it was better for me to do it; I thought, 'I'm his wife, it's my job.' It started our day off very stressfully – me pushing him into the shower and making him stay there while I washed him; me complaining to him about the mess when he spat toothpaste at the mirror; me yelling at him to 'Keep your bloody foot still!' while I wrestled with putting his socks on; me crying when he took the sock off one foot while I put his shoe on the other. It took more than an hour every day and it was exhausting.

If we had to go anywhere early, it also included shaving him and I would start preparing him around 6 am, even though his meds made him too sleepy to be able to manage it. It always felt like a fight, though we did *always* have a cuddle at the end of it and often laughed over it. At least that's how I remember it.

From the very first morning a carer came to take over that role, I discovered what a blessing it was. I thought Brian would not handle being naked with another woman, but as the carers came in uniform, he was accepting of a 'nurse'. He was his usual polite self in front of the carers and did not resist their instructions at all. They cleaned up his mess without complaint and never told him off if he was uncooperative. Familiarity really does allow contempt – it is that 'unconditional love' thing, and we both knew we would still love each other no matter how rude we were to each other in the mornings. Brian didn't feel familiarity or love for the professional carers, so he was just beautifully compliant.

While they attended to Brian, I had a quiet breakfast, read the paper and prepared his breakfast. After two years of hating waking up, our mornings became blissful overnight!

Initially we had carers attend five mornings a week to assist Brian. The two or three regular carers had a great routine. Once we got used to that assistance, we gratefully accepted some afternoon respite as well. I could use it to shop, exercise or just sit in the sun and read, and Brian could spend some time in the company of someone who would give him their undivided attention.

In the early days, I had workers come into my home for respite afternoons who would stick Brian in front of the television, watch him nap and spend the afternoon on their phones. Others would apologise for cleaning my refrigerator (yes, *apologise*!) because Brian had napped and they did not want to do nothing. One lovely lady put music on and danced with Brian – quite an achievement – and he would always be happy when I returned if he had spent the hour with her.

As a carer, I was reasonably confident that I was doing the best I could to look after the husband I loved. So I needed to feel that the professional carers who came into our home understood our needs and, most importantly, wanted to be there with him.

Community Options had provided us with personal and efficient service, but when the system for support changed and care packages were introduced, in 2013 we put our name down for a Level 4 package. A care package with HammondCare became available and I jumped to take it. It put our caring costs up tenfold per month and reduced our hours of help by about 25 per cent. The previous system was charged at the discretion of the provider but as the system changed, the new fees were fixed costs. We lost some time in the mornings as it was deemed that Brian would only need 30 minutes for help to shower and dress instead of the hour we were used to and, once on the package, we could only use one provider for all services. This reduced some of our respite options in the afternoon and also meant we lost those familiar carers who Brian thought of as friends. But we had been encouraged to take the package as the old system was being phased out.

I understood that changes to the things we were used to would need to be made, but change is terrifying for someone with dementia. That is almost the 'first rule' of dementia. The changes to our usual care workers who assisted Brian to dress and shower in the morning would take some getting used to as they learned the routine. It would also take time for Brian to learn again to trust strangers.

The HammondCare team took over and did things a bit differently, and an hour later in the mornings than we were used to. The first morning did not run smoothly and I ended up taking over as the carer could not get Brian to cooperate. She said he was a stronger man than she was used to. I was sure it would get better as we adjusted to the change. The second morning was no better, and neither was the third. Although the company prided itself on being the 'dementia specialists', I think their workers were primarily used to much older clients who were more frail and infirm than my strapping, six-foot-tall husband.

For outings, Brian liked to go out with a man rather than a woman. He wanted to talk about sport and war history. With a male carer, he felt like he was out with a mate when they went for coffee or a walk, while female companions made him feel like he was with a babysitter or cheating on me.

Previously, there had been a couple of male carers who Brian went out with regularly. Nandi was Hungarian, I think; he worked as a care worker and a massage therapist, was well read, and usually dressed in Thai fisherman pants. He was calm and caring and happy to share stories of his life with Brian. He gave Brian hand and foot massages. Brian felt very close to Nandi and looked forward to drives to the beach or walks in the escarpment with him. The other carer, Jim, was typical of the men Brian had known all his life and a rugby league tragic; they went on drives together and talked football the whole time. Nandi and Jim often took Brian out together with his friend David, who also had a form of dementia.

HammondCare only had one male carer in their employ locally, and he would be assigned to Brian for outings. Of course, I understood that he would not be available all the time. I hoped to introduce the new carer to Brian as a friend, so Brian would think he was part of my group of friends. We took a trip to the local pool, where I introduced him to Brian, and they shook hands.

Brian was used to coming to the pool with me and he was friendly with the staff who, wonderfully, would keep a bit of an eye on him as he paced around the grounds while I was in the water. Brian was also very familiar with the group I trained with, which included my younger brother, Greg. Brian used to swim too but it was never his favourite form of exercise, and he had by that stage forgotten how to swim. It had become dangerous for him to get into the water, and he no longer enjoyed that activity.

Our new carer seemed to have a lovely, caring attitude and I liked him straightaway. However, Brian was still athletic, and the new carer was soon exhausted following Brian around and around the pool for 40 minutes while I swam. We followed the swim, as usual, with a chat and a coffee with the group and Brian seemed happy seated beside his carer, who talked to him.

The following day, the carer arrived at our home in the afternoon. I had some shopping to do, so I suggested they walk to our local bakery, less than 500 metres away, to buy themselves afternoon tea, bring it home and watch a movie. I would be gone about 90 minutes. I waited for them to leave first, in case there was a problem, giving them five minutes before I got the car out of the garage.

We lived one street away from the main thoroughfare where the bakery was located. As I rounded the corner onto the main road, I could see Brian 300 metres ahead of me, running up the middle of the street. His poor carer was also running but was nowhere near Brian. He just couldn't keep up. I pulled up alongside Brian and asked him what he was doing. 'That bloke won't leave me alone,' he told me. 'I can't get away from him!'

I put Brian in the car and turned back to collect his worn-out carer, who was slumped against a telegraph pole. We drove to the bakery, purchased cake and returned home. I did not go shopping.

I telephoned my new case manager at HammondCare, who had assured me she would be available to discuss any concerns. She was on annual leave. Another staff member who knew nothing about Brian promised to get someone to call me.

A manager called me the next day. In tears I told her that nothing in this first week had gone smoothly and that Brian's care prior to this had been gentle and easy. I said I wished we had not taken the package and that I just wanted my old case manager at Community Options back. She dropped us like a hot potato!

Luckily for them (oh, I mean *us*), none of the paperwork had been completed due to the new case manager's annual leave. They refunded the money we had paid them, so the government department and HammondCare's hierarchy would be none the wiser.

Another Level 4 package did not become available for us before Brian's condition required palliative care, so we were able to resume our old ways, which was lucky for us. Community Options picked up where they had left off and life returned to 'normal'.

The philosophy of care providers and their staff is fantastic. Most of the workers in the care sector are dedicated and tireless, and we met some extraordinary people on this journey. If not for this book, I probably wouldn't even be able to recall the bad times.

But the practice of some care organisations, in times of real need, falls way short of their ethos.

Dear HammondCare, and almost all dementia care services,
Please try to live up to your advertising.

Your theories are fantastic, but my experience of your practice doesn't give me confidence in your claims.

Being able to provide for frail, elderly people with dementia does not make you 'dementia specialists'. Your carers need to be able to look after a fit, strong man who gets frustrated and cannot express himself.

Give me a break – please, someone, *give me a break!*

SEVENTEEN

A sensational service

In the last seven last years of Brian's life, we battled a care system full of theories and good intentions, and care providers who could not provide the services they said they could. The one *great* service we found was Carunya. It was a dementia day centre that did not feel clinical, or like a hospital or nursing home. Those environments filled Brian with the fear of being investigated, further diagnosed or abandoned.

Instead, Carunya provided Brian with friends who were his peers, activities suited to his needs, and a safe and familiar environment. It emulated the kind of 'club' atmosphere he was used to.

The staff were exceptional. They understood the peculiar behaviours associated with dementia and were able to effectively manage those behaviours. Several times they went far beyond my expectations to help Brian to ensure *he* was happy.

Brian loved visiting Carunya once a week. He couldn't tell me what he liked about it, just that they did 'stuff' there. There was very little 'stuff' that Brian and I could do – I found it very hard to keep his attention – but the Carunya staff were sensational at it.

For me, it was the only respite opportunity I had where I was confident that he was in safe hands, and would come home happy and calm.

Years later, during Covid, Carunya was closed down by the area health service; its staff were redeployed and another service was moved to the building. When other services closed during Covid restrictions gradually reopened, Carunya did not.

The partners and carers of people with dementia who had been using Carunya were not happy, and Mary Paris, whose husband used the service, organised a protest meeting and asked me to speak as a carers' advocate. I don't mind a bit of public speaking and was delighted to be able to help.

'In a time when aged and disability care systems are screaming for reform and funding it is incomprehensible to me that Illawarra Shoalhaven Local Health District could consider closing such an innovative and effective service,' I said in my speech to the group, which included the health service's executive director of clinical operations. 'I believe the values of openness and respect for Carunya's clients were not considered at all.' I wanted the health service to understand how I felt about Carunya at the time Brian was attending.

I was not the only speaker on the day and our point was collectively and successfully made. The following year, Carunya reopened and Mary Paris's partner, Stewart West, went straight back in the door as if nothing had changed.

In my speech, I also read out a thank you letter I had written to Robert and Paula – the nursing administrators who operated the centre. But the best people and services aren't remembered by me because of these letters. They are remembered by me because they still sit in my heart.

Dear Robert and Paula,
Thank you for your perseverance.

When you both came to suggest Brian start attending Carunya, he was rude and uncooperative. Although I said we would give it a try, he told me he did not want to go.

When the bus arrived the first Monday morning to pick him up, he was not impressed and I am not sure how I got him on it.

I know from the debrief I received after his morning there that he was angry and rude and even threw his water bottle – not behaviour that is allowed there – but you agreed to give him a second go.

I now know that he was scared that I had put him into a facility from which he could not come home. He saw it as the beginning of the end.

The second week, when he would not get on the bus, I was resigned to it being a failure but you were kind enough to send someone he knew to pick him up in a car and he happily went with Jim to have a 'free lunch'. He came home again with Jim in a good mood. Jim picked him up the third week, but he came home on the bus with a big smile on his face.

Now he goes happily on the bus and is asking nearly every day when he can go again.

It is so hard to occupy Brian. I wish I could make him that happy at home.

Thank you for not giving up on him and thank you for organising something that he can enjoy.

EIGHTEEN

The bloody awful week

I am a bit of an organiser. I like to plan so things run smoothly. You know the sort of thing: putting aside enough time to get ready for a function; pre-cooking meals if guests will be staying at the house; packing a bag of coloured pencils, paper, books and Lego on a car trip with children. The ordinary things we do to make life run smoothly.

Schemes don't always run to plan, of course, but when life is relatively normal, you just adjust and fight the little fires as they come up.

When your life is not all your own, even the smallest of problems sabotage what might have looked like a meticulous plan.

Dear outside world, service providers and retail salespersons – everyone who doesn't live with me, in fact! What a bloody awful week we've had.

Monday
I used my respite time to purchase a new washing machine as mine broke down on Saturday. (Brian cannot manage to go into shops anymore.) It had only been two days without a

machine, but now that Brian is not able to toilet himself, our washing involves soiled clothes, towels and linen – not things I can handwash!

I did my research online and had a fair idea of which machine I wanted to buy.

One store gave me a good price. I should have been happy with that but now that we are living on a pension I thought I would try to get it cheaper. Another store did not have the same machine but the charming sales assistant showed me a different machine that did all the same things, had a five-year warranty and was $300 cheaper. She gave me free delivery as I was a pensioner, and I left there very happy. I went and got our groceries.

Although the shopping took too much of my time to go for a swim, I felt quite relaxed.

Brian arrived home from an outing to Carunya, happy and very tired. He slept on the couch for two hours, but woke so confused and angry I had to give him a whole risperidone tablet – he usually only has half.

Tuesday

Tuesday morning rolled around and we got ready for a new activity group meeting – the first one for the year – at a local museum. Brian seemed 'hungover' from the extra medication and getting ready was a bit harder than usual.

He wanted to get in the shower but kept getting back into bed. Once in the shower, he wanted out before he was washed. He got back into bed when I asked him to sit on the end of it so I could begin to dress him. He ate breakfast with very little help, so I thought everything was okay, but when it was time to go to the toilet he refused and got quite cross with me. He glared at me when I was cleaning his teeth and told me off. He spat toothpaste all over the bench. He had wee'd on the toilet floor and would not let me clean his shoes before he walked through the house (thank heavens for tiles)!

Just as we were leaving for the meeting, Nandi, one of

our carers, arrived up at the house. There had been an administrative mix-up and Nandi had not known that service had ceased. I confirmed with him that Brian would have a carer pick him up on Friday and we went our separate ways. Unfortunately Brian wanted to go with Nandi and not me, and became quite agitated in the car. By the time we got to Wollongong he was shouting at me that I was in the wrong place and was kicking the wall of the car at his feet. He calmed down when he saw our friends outside the museum and greeted them with the type of smile he used to give me.

He found the museum boring, and there was a scary ten minutes when he had to come downstairs from a display. It was my fault – I never should have let him go upstairs. I thought the poor woman who was escorting us was going to have a heart attack waiting for him to fall. I just wanted to tell her to shut up when she kept giving you instructions. (Just what Brian needed: another naggy voice!) He enjoyed lunch and even walked happily back with me to the car.

The washing machine arrived quite late on Tuesday afternoon.

I carefully read the instructions (not real hard), plugged in pipes and electrics and started on four days' worth of washing. Water immediately began to run out the base of the machine and all over the floor. I quickly turned it off and called the store – which of course was now shut.

Wednesday

I called again first thing Wednesday morning and another charming sales assistant said he would arrange a refund and to pick up the machine. He would call me back with details. I called him again three hours later; he acted surprised that no one had contacted me. He told me to wait at home between 3 and 6 pm and the machine would be picked up.

I asked him to put the refund directly back to my credit card. No, he said, I had to come into the store (not happy!). I explained that the only time I could come was between 1 and 4 pm, but he wouldn't do that either as I still had the machine.

I rearranged an appointment and an outing with friends and waited in. No one picked up the machine.

Brian was taken out by a carer but I had to stay home. I sent an email to the store's head office.

Thursday

I called the store just after 9 am and asked to speak to the franchisee in whitegoods. He said, 'Oh, you must be the lady who sent a complaint about us.' That filled me with confidence – he had the complaint but had not yet called me. He did not apologise for any inconvenience so far but promised to make pick-up arrangements and call me back.

Brian was out with a friend for two hours but, again, I was stuck at home waiting for the call.

I called him after four hours had passed. He was out. He called an hour later and said he would call me back. A delivery driver called half an hour later and promised to pick it up between 2 and 4 pm – and he did.

Of course, in the meantime, I still had to buy a new machine. I rang the first store I'd approached and arranged the delivery over the phone – no delivery fee, no installation costs, arrived on time, works beautifully. Now I have paid for two machines – lucky we have unlimited income (not)!

I did feel a lot less stressed once the faulty machine was picked up, and knew I could have three hours respite on Friday afternoon, when Brian was collected by a carer. Knowing I would be able to pick up the refund and then go for a much-needed swim was a comfort.

Friday

Brian and I were out briefly in the morning, and we came home to have lunch and get ready for him to be collected at 12.30. No one came.

I telephoned the service provider, who said the service had been cancelled by our case manager. I explained that they only facilitated the service on Tuesdays and that a different provider facilitated the Friday service, which was to go on. They hurriedly called a carer and arranged for Brian to still be collected.

A nice lady named Rebecca arrived an hour later but Brian was asleep. He always wakes a little confused from a nap and because he did not know the new carer, he was not really interested in going anywhere with her. I explained that I needed to pick up the washing machine refund and that Rebecca would take him to buy ice cream. He went out to her car, a ute, but then he could not work out how to climb up and into it. After a few attempts he just got angry and refused to try again.

I suggested they stay home while I went to get the refund and that I would return with ice creams. Brian got so angry I thought he was going to hit out at me, so I gave him a half a risperidone – his normal dose, but three hours early. Rebecca agreed to come with me and sit in the car with Brian so I could at least pick up the money – otherwise I wouldn't get another chance until next week.

The refund procedure took three people and 20 minutes. The round trip took 45 minutes. Then Rebecca left.

I am in dire need of a break and Brian is in desperate need of some stimulation. I guess we wait until next week for that now.

I feel so abandoned when things go wrong. They tell me I need to look after myself but when the wheels fall off, there is no one to help.

So ... to everyone else in the world: none of you can have even an inkling of what is going on in someone else's life. Your actions have consequences. When you are dealing with people, please check to see if the easiest thing for you creates the hardest thing for them.

Just 7 per cent of the week belongs exclusively to me. Please let me have that time each week to do what I need to do.

Wedding, March 1979, aged 20 and 22.

*Brian in action. St George Rugby Leagues
First Grade Fullback, 1979–1985.*

Our family complete, Christmas Day, 1992.

Backpacking in Europe 1987, Photo at the top of the Jungfrau, Switzerland – a picnic in the snow.

Our last day out walking together across the Lawrence Hargrave Bridge, Stanwell Park, NSW, in 2015.

Brian's last months.

A family portrait, taken just after Brian's dementia diagnosis.

Head Coach of Rugby League, Australian Institute of Sport.

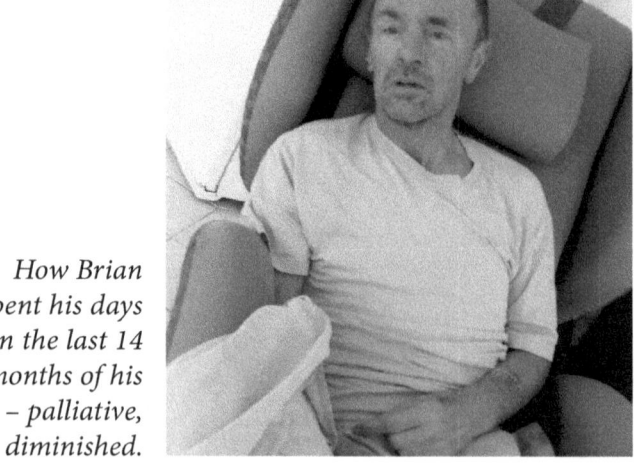

How Brian spent his days in the last 14 months of his life – palliative, diminished.

Brian's "Band of Brothers": Grant, Alan, Garry, Peter, Brian and Doug.

St George First Grade Reunion. Team mates caring for him, 2014 – Graeme Wynn, Bruce Starkey, Graham Quinn, John Jansen, George Grant, Brian Johnson, Michael Sorridimi.

Head Coach, Warrington Rugby League Club, England, 1988 to 1996.

NINETEEN

Band of brothers

When you are at home and isolated dealing with a problem, it is too easy to imagine that the outside world is having a wonderful time with not a care in the world. But everyone has something going on. People cannot give their friends the time that they need to give to their own families and problems, especially at an age when we still have full-time jobs, children living at home and elderly parents who need time and care. There are lawns to mow, board meetings to attend, houses to clean and holidays to take, in between going to work and giving time to our own partners.

But Brian and I have been blessed with wonderful friends, so many of whom found time in their hectic lives to help us. Just to sit and talk with them salvaged my mental health on countless occasions. Being able to share our struggles lessened the weight of those struggles.

We have several circles of friends, as everyone does: friends from schooldays, from rugby league, from our work. The men and women Brian met at teachers' college back in the mid-1970s have remained close friends for almost 50 years, and there is a group of five who I think of as the most important of these men from his teachers' college days: Garry Posetti, Grant Mairs, Doug Hearne, Peter Hickey and Paul Ghiradello. We met in our late teens and over the ensuing years, through changing relationships and the tragedy of divorce, I was eventually the only 'original' woman left. Now all the wives just have to accept me as I think of their husbands as my brothers. Brian certainly considered them his brothers, and they proved they were his brothers during his final years.

I know how lucky Brian and I were (and I still am) to have this band of brothers.

Garry Posetti, Brian's very closest mate, was my rock. As the owner of a business, he works six days a week, and when Brian became ill he was an only son giving care and time to his elderly mother. He has three adult children who he spends lots of time and energy with and he is also a loving, caring partner. Yet … when I had to go to hospital for a couple of days, he moved into our home to care for Brian overnight and in the mornings before a carer arrived to look after him during the day. He had dinner with us several times a week. He rang every day.

Garry's nickname is 'Mr Make it Happen', as he is the event organiser in our group. He never left us out of an invitation to a group dinner or concert – even though Brian might need to be fed like a child in a restaurant or might make a scene in public.

Grant Mairs is another of this close-knit group and now lives in Canberra. In the last 14 months of Brian's life, when Brian was bedridden and had virtually no language skills, Grant came every second weekend, without fail, and stayed with us. One weekend, he arrived with Peter Fitzsimons' book *Fromelles and Pozières*. Brian's biggest interest outside of rugby league had always been World War I history, ever since his teenage years. He loved the books written by Les Carlyon and Peter Fitzsimons, among others, on the subject. Grant read to Brian from that book for hours.

He walked with me when I had a respite carer, and sometimes he *was* the respite carer. Other mates and sometimes their partners would join us for dinner on Friday evenings. I am so grateful to

Grant for the time he gave us, and I am so very grateful to his wife, my lovely friend Brenda, who loaned him to us every second weekend for 14 months.

It was remiss of me, I realise as I wade through my letters, to not have written my thank yous to these fabulous friends – my brothers. I hope I told them at them at the time.

I did write to one wonderful friend: a business friend, Chris Stylis. Brian and I had known him for a long time – he was the management agent who looked after our rented home when we lived in England.

While taking Brian to the movies, I saw Chris and his wife Sharon just ahead of us in the line to buy tickets. Chris came over and said he had just heard of Brian's illness, and he asked me to call him if there was anything he could do for us. It was a very sincere offer that had been made by many of our friends and acquaintances, and they all meant it. But I did not know what anyone could do.

One Sunday afternoon, a month or so later, Chris knocked on our door.

'You're never going to ask me to do anything, are you?' he said. 'Well, I've decided what I will do. I'll pick Brian up every Friday morning and take him out for a walk and a coffee so you can have a couple of hours to yourself.'

I tried to explain to him that Brian needed assistance to eat and drink, and that it caused other problems out in public because he needed assistance to go to the toilet. Chris laughed at me and told me he knew how to help someone do those things because he had done those things for his children when they were small, and it would not be any big deal. I could not dissuade him, although I suggested once a fortnight instead of once a week.

Chris arrived the first Friday in his beautifully cut suit and shiny dress shoes and took Brian, in his slip-on shoes and tracksuit pants, to Kiama to walk along the beachfront and share a coffee before he went to his office. He did this for months until Brian's ability to get in and out of the car, and his agitation within the car, made it impossible.

Those two hours a fortnight were a beautiful and unexpected gift to Brian and me. Brian looked forward to the trip out, and I had time to do some extra shopping, or to go for a swim or walk on my own.

There were so many times during those last years when friends stepped up and gave me help and time and understanding that was generous and loving.

I am so grateful to them all.

Dear Chris,

Thank you, thank you, thank you.

I cannot say that enough.

You have set up regular contact with Brian, and that contact is invaluable to both him and me.

Your kindness to him – especially as he declines – is unexpected and gratefully received.

I see it getting harder for you to sustain but I will accept your kindness until you feel you cannot do it anymore.

Brian looks forward to his outings with you and often asks in the interim if you are coming today.

You are a true gentleman and one of the most genuine people I have ever met!

TWENTY

Respite? Not quite

Note to Self

I think it is time to start taking the advice given to carers: 'Look after yourself.'

I don't think I am depressed, but …

The winter hasn't been any fun. I don't want to swim or even go for a walk. I am living on comfort food. When was the last time I ate a vegetable? Respite time is completely wasted grocery shopping and sitting in coffee shops alone. I have sciatica. I cannot be bothered socialising – I have nothing to say to anyone. My studies have gone to pot. Nothing fits me. Blah blah blah.

I think it's time to stop whinging and do something about it.

Carers talk constantly about the mythical 'overnight respite'. I know the chances of getting it now are even slimmer than when I needed it, but in ten months I have had two nights off. It's time to call the respite service and have some serious time to myself.

I will do it on Monday and record the result!

When Brian was still relatively mildly affected by dementia, he was offered an overnight stay at a cottage a few suburbs from our house. Other men from our support group were also attending so I thought he might have a good time and tried to 'sell' it to him as a 'boys' weekend away'. He did not want to go but said he would as David, Ian and Mike would be there too.

The schedule for the weekend included a trip to a museum, coffee and morning tea out, and a walk on the beach. I was familiar with the cottage so I knew he would be safe and comfortable, and I suspected he would not recognise the neighbourhood so would not try to come home.

As the day approached, the provider contacted me and said they would be moving to a cottage in Dapto. It is just around the corner from our house. I knew Brian would know exactly where he was and that he would not be happy.

The provider talked me around, encouraging me to take some 'me time'. I knew I needed a break in the day and a good night's sleep, so I accepted the offer.

I was right. Brian knew exactly where he was and set his sights on coming home. He managed to scale the garden wall but was caught and returned inside. That meant no one else could have access to the garden for the whole weekend.

His museum trip was to an automobile museum, again close to our home. Brian was less interested in cars than anyone I have ever met. He was not impressed.

The provider coped with his attempts to abscond, and his anger and boredom, and did not call me at all. I had a nice 32-hour break, and did not find out about the problems until after the event.

Brian made me promise not to do it to him again.

About two years later, when he was much less able, we were again offered a few days in a respite cottage. I declined, but this provider was very persuasive, and I was encouraged by family and friends to take up the offer.

The cottage was on the water, about an hour and a half south of where we live. Brian would only be staying with people he was familiar with, and there would only be four guests. Mike, Eila and David were members of our dementia support group and I was also very friendly with their caring partners: Gail, Alan and Jenny. They would play ball games, go for picnics and walks, and be very comfortable in their own ensuite rooms in a cottage with nice grounds and directly opposite a park.

It did not end well.

Dear service provider of cottage respite,

Oh, how wonderful you seemed when you rang last May to offer Brian four nights in a cottage near the water. I had my reservations but then spoke to people whose partners had stayed there and had had a lovely time.

I got a little concerned when, a week from the date, I had still not had any confirmation, so I emailed to check. I was assured that it was on and that someone would call me with details in a day or two. I booked a night in a Sydney hotel, and tickets for Brett and I to go to the theatre.

A young lady rang me last Wednesday to check on Brian's medications. I explained that I would also send down a bottle of chocolate sauce because I always crush his tablets and give them to him on a spoon of sauce, as he cannot swallow whole tablets. She was horrified! They could not do that. It was against policy. Some tablets are slow-release, she said, and not meant to be crushed.

I explained that I had cleared the crushing of his tablets with his doctors and none of them was slow release. She rang her supervisor. No. Against policy. I explained that it would take a lot of time and water to get Brian to take his tablets any other way. She said that was their job and they had techniques.

I felt like an incompetent carer who could not even give him tablets correctly and bowed to her better judgement. I had become so distracted by the medications that I forgot to ask any other details.

The following day, I realised that they had not asked anything about Brian's food preferences and emailed just to let them know he did not drink milk, he drank his coffee black, and I would include a carton of almond milk for his cereal. Brian is very easy to feed. He just likes food. So it did not seem important to mention anything else.

I had not given Brian a lot of details about his trip. He knew he was going for a weekend down the coast with his friends Eila, David and Mike. He knew he had a packed bag and would be staying overnight. When Alan picked him up on Friday morning he was excited and almost ran to the car.

I came inside, washed floors, packed an overnight bag and set off for Sydney. I took my time driving up, stopping to mooch in a couple of shops on the way and stopped for a sandwich. I was at the hotel by three. Met Brett for a walk and coffee then we had an early dinner in Dixon Street, a cocktail at the hotel bar and went to see a play. I slept well, had a room service breakfast in bed (luxury) and met two of my cousins for a long lunch in the city. I rushed back to Bulli for a wine-tasting dinner with friends and slept in on Sunday morning. It was Liam's birthday and Father's Day, so I was looking forward to a family lunch at a local club when the phone rang at 10 am.

A care worker from the cottage said that Brian was upset and 'looked aggressive'. Would I please speak to him on the phone? I asked him if he was having a nice time. He yelled 'Fuck that!' and I said I'd be there as soon as I could. There was no way I could placate him. Especially over the phone. I suggested to the worker that he distract him with a bowl of ice cream or some chocolate and I would leave home as soon as I could.

I rang to give my apologies for the family lunch, woke Liam and gave him his birthday present, apologised for not being able to spend some time with him and set off to the cottage.

By the time I got there, Brian was calm and smiling. His face lit up when he saw me. 'Are you having a nice time?' I asked him.

'It's nice now that you are here,' he told me.

While a care worker was getting Brian's bag from another room (he couldn't get it quick enough!), Eila told me that Brian had been very upset and had fallen over, and the ambulance had come. I was astounded to find this out from Eila. The worker said the staff had called an ambulance because they couldn't get Brian up off the floor. It was just a small tumble with no injury – no big deal. He handed me a bag of wet clothes that hadn't had time to dry. Then he ushered me out to the car.

I could have pursued the fall and ambulance story but decided that I would wait to call the office on Monday so as not to cause a scene or disrupt the others' weekend. I did not look at the wet clothes and just assumed that Brian had dropped food on them.

He was asleep as soon as he sat in the car and he slept, deeply, all the way home. I could tell he had not slept well the night before. I assumed that was why he had been upset and 'looked aggressive' – he gets cranky if he's tired. (So do I.)

As soon as we got home, I took him to the toilet. I was astounded to find he was wearing incontinence pants. I checked the wet clothes bag. Trousers, underpants and pyjamas. It was obvious Brian had wet his pants and his bed. This could only happen if no one had taken him to the toilet. His urine was very dark – I'd never seen urine that dark before – and I guessed he was also dehydrated. What – no drinks, either?

I made him a sandwich and he went to sleep eating it. I moved him to the couch and he slept for two hours.

My parents called around and I took him to the toilet. Luckily my mum is experienced – she identified the blood in his urine. By this time I was cross! I needed to take him to the doctor so I needed the information on his fall. Luckily the support worker who had arranged the respite answered her mobile. She explained that Brian had gone to sit in a chair the afternoon before and had missed it, landing on the floor. The ambulance had come to help him up and check he was okay. Brian ate dinner so no one was concerned. She said he probably had a urinary tract infection.

The doctor at the medical centre was lovely and very patient with Brian (and me – because he could tell I was stressed!). He tested a urine sample and confirmed that Brian had a lot of blood in it, but that the white blood cells were too low to suggest an infection. He would treat him for an infection anyway and send the sample for further testing. He thought Brian needed an ultrasound on his kidneys and prostate and would send the results to our usual GP.

Brian barely slept on Sunday night. On Monday he was out of bed before 5 am and spent the morning pacing at double time around the house. A worker picked him up and took him to Carunya at 10 am.

I had an appointment to see a doctor on a different matter but couldn't contain myself and cried like a baby in her office. I did nap in the afternoon, which was lucky because I needed extra strength when they bought my psychotic, cranky husband home.

He was like a whirling dervish. He would not sit down for his usual afternoon nap and paced through the house punching furniture, and kicking doors and the kitchen bin. I tried the usual distractions – ice cream and hand holding – but he was too angry even for ice cream. He told me he was punching chairs so he would not hurt anyone.

Brian threw and smashed his trophy from the AIS.

Liam found dealing with these outbursts difficult and was not able to help me. I rang his sister Narelle for help, and slipped Brian another half of risperidone.

By the time Narelle arrived, Brian was little calmer and I was able to give him dinner. He was very happy to see his sister, which helped a lot. After dinner I was able to get him into bed for a reasonably early night and the extra tablet made sure he slept.

We went to see our GP on Tuesday morning. Brian was still agitated and pacing. The doctor checked the sample results and found no infection but kept him on the antibiotics 'just in case'. He also prescribed Ativan as a last resort for his anger. Lucky – because Tuesday night saw him just as psychotic.

A support worker from the cottage respite provider came to visit on Wednesday morning. The worker at the cottage had denied not knowing details of the people he was looking after and denied telling me that. They had excuses for Brian's wet bed and fall, but basically they were not up to caring for him.

I had kept my concerns to myself over the weekend and did not let the partners of the other three friends staying at the cottage know of the problems I had discovered on his return. Now I regret that.

Mike, who also has dementia and is a paraplegic, returned home with pressure sores; his crotch was red raw. His wife, Gail, doubted that he had been out of his chair even to sleep and was sure he had not been showered for the five days he was there. Their doctor wanted to put him in to hospital until the sores were healed. He had also been extremely upset and had wanted to go home but when Gail had spoken to him over the phone, she'd thought he was just a little homesick.

So, service provider, why are you offering a service you are not up to?

You had a care plan for Brian that was 13 months old. You provide some care to him each week. Did your notes from his care workers each week not show you the level of care he now requires? Are your staff not trained to take someone to the toilet? Aren't your people obligated to let me know if my husband has a fall severe enough to require an ambulance?

I think there must be very good profit from government subsidies to offer this service. It is far from client focused.

It is inadequate.

TWENTY-ONE

Aftershocks

The outcome for Brian's four days away had not been good. Not for Brian. Not for me. Not for Mike, who had also been there, and not for his wife Gail.

Gail was keen to get legal advice, but I was just too tired. Even if I had been able to establish the service provider was at fault, there was nothing I could do to get Brian back, emotionally, to where he had been before that weekend.

I don't know if he remembered what happened. He certainly could not give me his side of the story. But he became fearful of strangers and people in uniform. He became fearful of me. He had his guard up, all the time, from that day on.

Many care workers after that time described him as 'aggressive'. He was never aggressive. He was defensive and reactionary. He had good reason to be. He could no longer trust anyone. He no longer trusted me.

For six months, wonderful nursing staff had come to us every morning to shower and dress Brian. Brian had always been pleased to see them arrive – and so was I. He was always polite and cooperative, and welcomed them with a big smile. He declined quite a bit in that time, but the regular workers knew him well enough to roll with the changes.

From the first day after his return from the cottage respite, he would not tolerate any of the workers, and pushed them away and swore at them. He refused to get into the shower cubicle and was uncooperative as they tried to dress him. Each of them commented on how vulnerable and frightened he seemed. He told me they were trying to kill him. By the fourth day, I had no choice but to cancel the service – I was doing it anyway while the care workers could only stand and watch.

Brian had always loved the activity centre at Carunya. It was his favourite outing of the week. About a week after his return from the cottage, he was due to attend again. He was his usual impatient self as he waited for the bus to pick him up, and perhaps a little more anxious than usual; he had had an angst-ridden week, pacing at double-quick time through the house and reacting angrily to any touch if he took his eyes off me. He still seemed so very vulnerable.

At around 2 pm, Carunya called to say Brian was too upset to get on the bus – would I come and pick him up instead? When I got there, they would not let me in the door, saying he was too aggressive and it would be too dangerous for me to go to him. They had called an ambulance – he was psychotic, and had fallen and hit his head.

I demanded to be let in. As soon as he saw me, he calmed. He looked exhausted. He was leaning over to the left and was only upright because he was against a wall. I held his hand and agreed to wait for the ambulance. Then they told me they had called the police to control him. I burst into tears. What would they do? Taser him? I walked him out of the building and helped him onto a stretcher with the police standing by. They were understanding, really, but I was wary.

At the hospital, Brian was shouting abuse and did not want anyone to come near him. A security guard arrived. I had to tell him to go away – it wasn't as though he was going to be kind and calm Brian down. The dementia nurse came to talk to me. She told me not to let Brian stay overnight; she felt that, no matter what training the staff said they had had, his care would not be good.

He had blood tests, X-rays and a brain scan, and then I insisted on bringing him home. The tests found nothing – just dementia. Carunya let me know he could not come back.

In that week, he started to refuse to go to the toilet. On the day he held on for 14 hours, I called another ambulance and he went to Wollongong Hospital. They were lovely, and the tests found nothing – just dementia. He finally went for a wee and we went home.

He had just been frightened to go into the toilet.

Memories might fade quickly but emotions don't. Feelings remain. Brian felt dread and despair. All I wanted was for him to feel calm and loved.

That particular company and that cottage were closed after Gail followed up her complaints on Mike's treatment over that week. The closure was done quietly, and could have been for several reasons but Gail is sure her official complaint was the straw that broke the camel's back.

The cottage did reopen under another name some time later. To me, a different name meant their reputation was cause for a much-needed rebranding.

I know that all sectors of the caring community are under-staffed and overworked, but individuals require focused and individual care. I knew exactly what Brian required, and the refusal of some care providers to listen to me about his needs, possible problems and solutions was short-sighted, as well as demoralising and disrespectful – to Brian and to me.

Dear service provider of cottage respite,

It is now more than two months since the respite weekend.

In that time, all Brian's regular services have had to be cancelled, you've had an internal 'investigation' (whitewash) of the incident, and, according to you it is a coincidence that Brian has changed so much since the weekend your staff were looking after him.

The investigation was relayed to me over the phone. Essentially, you decided that my husband was a naughty boy who did not know how to follow your procedures and ruined the weekend for everyone else. Your staff were all adequately trained and no one hurt him, you told me – even though he had bruises down his side and was weeing blood. There was nothing in the notes, you said, so nothing happened.

Not only that, but you told me a man with similar care needs to Brian who had been attending the cottage happily for months could no longer attend because of a new policy on high-care clients that was implemented after Brian's stay. The implied message was that it was all my fault that this man's life was now ruined.

You checked that I hadn't initiated any legal processes. I hadn't. And that was the end of it.

Thank you. I lost all my services, Brian lost all his outings, and your service did nothing wrong. Nice one.

TWENTY-TWO

The Happiness Project, part 2

Caring is hard work. Watching someone die, incrementally, every day is soul destroying. I tried to remain happy and to make him happy.

It did not always work.

Several times, when I felt low, I tried to make lists of happiness. It was a bit futile sometimes, helpful at other times.

Dear Brian,

I haven't written a letter for while – I only seem to write about sad stuff and it was depressing me!

More and more you are unhappy, and I keep forgetting our pledge to look for the joy in our lives.

This will be an ongoing list – every day I will add to it. New month, new list. Here goes!

1 April 2014

Made love this morning, for the first time in a month – not like of old, but we were close. I could feel the love we have – that we have always had. I love you.

Later in the morning, Alan and Eila came for morning tea. I heard them on our driveway and went to greet them. Eila got out of the car and rushed over to me with a very concerned look on her face. She said she heard that I had fallen – was I okay? I assured her I was and that I hadn't fallen. She was insistent and appeared very worried.

Then she took my hand and said, 'What day is it today?' I said it was Tuesday. She said, 'No, it is a special day', and laughed. I twigged: April Fools' Day. She laughed very hard – she got me! She was joyful! It made me happy too. Eila, despite her dementia, knows how to look for joy – I hope I can keep hold of the little lesson she gave me. If she can be happy, then I am sure I can be.

6 April 2014

Swam in the Shellharbour Surf Club Ocean Swim today. I beat my time from last year by 14 minutes. Not as miraculous as it sounds – I wore flippers this year. We had a small family team including my brother, our nephews and cousins. It was a great day, and you enjoyed it as much as I did. During the swim I saw lots of little blue-and-yellow-striped fish and no sharks – lots of joy in that!

26 April 2014

Why haven't I written anything for 20 days? Have I been miserable? No way.

We went to our goddaughter Mandy's wedding – joyous from start to finish and we danced!

Last weekend, Brett was home and Grant stayed over. We went for a lovely walk. I cooked a special dinner – beef in red wine and chocolate. We walked again on Sunday morning. too.

Tonight was your St George first-grade reunion. You had a wonderful time – you hadn't been so happy in weeks.

I need to keep this list up! There are happy things in almost every one of our days. No matter how small I must acknowledge them. I want to feel happy – I want to make *you* feel happy. It is the only way to keep us content to be together. Concentrate, Karen, you dill!

16 November 2014

Gosh … what happened to the joy I wanted to write about?

I haven't done this in more than six months.

Has there been no joy?

It feels that way.

We haven't made love since April!

You cannot talk to me anymore.

You're not happy. I'm not happy.

I don't feel like your wife anymore. Just your carer. I am sad that I have let it get to this, but I don't see a way back.

It just gets harder and harder.

TWENTY-THREE

Joyce

Brian and I were not the only people affected by his disease. Our sons lost their dad. Narelle and Debbie lost their calm sensible big brother, who they had often looked to for advice. Brian's elderly mum, Joyce, lost her caring and supportive son.

Joyce was also suffering from dementia. She lived independently, with daily assistance from both Debbie and Narelle, until it became too difficult to care for her at home and she moved to a local nursing home.

I felt it was easier to fool her about Brian's condition than tell her the truth. Only once did I relent. We were eating lunch together, and Joyce saw Brian struggling with his cutlery. 'Why is he doing that?' she asked me.

'Because he has been diagnosed with dementia,' I told her.

'Rubbish!' she scoffed, 'That's what they told *me*, and I don't have it!'

A few minutes later, she again asked me why Brian was doing something she had noticed was a bit odd. I just shrugged.

After Brian died, Joyce would sometimes ask where he was. I always said he was working, or that he was in France with the AIS rugby league team. She accepted that. I never found the courage to tell her he was gone. I did not want to make her cry. What was the point? No parent wants to know they have outlived their child.

Dear Joyce,

When you first went into the nursing home, I came nearly every day and sat with you for an hour or so. I always brought some knitting or crocheting with me so we could pass the time doing it together. Occasionally Brian came with me but he began to feel uncomfortable there. Now he doesn't want to come at all. Lately I haven't been able to come either. I am so sorry.

I was quite shocked on Sunday when I saw you for the first time in three weeks. You are repeating yourself even more than you were last time I saw you.

You were obviously worried about Brian. I know you told Narelle that he looked 'doddery' and it concerned you.

Debbie wants me to tell you about his condition. She thinks you have a right to know because you are his mum. There are lots of things we don't tell you because they will cause you distress. This is just one of them. You probably have a right to know that your house has been sold, too, but no one is going to tell you that!

I can tell you that he loved seeing you on Sunday. He sat with you the whole time we were there and did not want to move from your side. I heard him tell you that he loves you. I wish he could spend more time with you. I wish he could be your big strong son again and bring you some comfort – I know how proud of him you are. And I wish you could be his mum again and help look after him.

I am sad for the two of you. I keep you apart only to lessen the distress. I'm sorry.

TWENTY-FOUR

On the home front

As Brian's dementia progressed, an occupational therapist recommended we make some modifications to our home. As Brian had an assessment under the Aged Care Scheme at the time, we qualified for some subsidised alterations to mitigate the risk of falls and ensure his physical safety.

He was having trouble with his depth perception and balance, and the simple task of stepping up to get over the threshold of our front and back doors was becoming too difficult for him. His foot would hit the front of the small step and he would trip into the doorway. He also had problems getting in and out of our shower cubicle; again, he would stumble over the small step. The risk of falling was becoming very real in even the simplest situations.

The stairs in our two-storey house were also becoming a nightmare. Brian would try to walk sideways down the stairs facing the banisters and, laying both hands on the rail, he would slowly descend, hand over hand. While his left hand was on the rail, he would take a step down then cross his right hand over … then immediately he would turn, because of the position of his right hand, and begin to walk back up the stairs. He was so frightened of falling he would not allow me to help.

On one occasion, my brother Ian and his family were visiting us from Perth. Ian listened to me ranting at Brian for 20 minutes as I tried to get him downstairs. In the end, Brian was back on the upstairs landing and I was in tears. Ian and his son Todd came to help and effectively carried Brian downstairs.

We installed railings and black rubber ramps so Brian could get in and out of the house without falling anymore. Rails were added to our upstairs shower and he was able to hold on as I got him in and out. But by then the stair problem had got so bad that we were sleeping downstairs and I was washing him using the laundry tub.

We had our downstairs bathroom measured up and six months later the modifications were finally complete. My advice to anyone who needs modifications is to push to get them done before you are completely desperate for them. The wheels of bureaucracy move slowly but for us, the eventual outcome was worth the wait.

Dear Scope Home Access,

Thank you, thank you, thank you for my beautiful new bathroom!

By the time it was installed, I was at my wits' end.

Four months after our bathroom was measured up, the approval for our modifications still had not gone through. It was getting harder and harder to get Brian up and down the stairs, and when I talked to friends about it, they suggested I call you and put some pressure on. I did not want to be pushy, so I waited.

After Brian's horrible cottage respite weekend, I called you, crying. The stairs were almost impossible, Brian was refusing to get into the shower or go into the small toilet, and I was having to take him to shopping centres and use disabled-access toilets so he had enough room not to be scared. We had moved our bed downstairs and I was giving him sponge baths in the laundry.

Finally, the contracts were ready to be signed, and four weeks later the work started.

The first part of the work was to knock out our existing downstairs toilet and laundry. What a nightmare! I was giving Brian sponge baths on a plastic chair by the kitchen sink, and chasing him around the house with a bucket and a commode. Using the commode was beyond him, and I found myself cleaning shit up off the floor in the kitchen, the bedroom/study and the lounge room. I joked about it at the time, but I have never felt so stressed.

But do you know what? It was all worth it. The design of the bathroom is sensational. It looks lovely. Now I can take Brian to a big room and shower him down when needed. So much easier than the kitchen sink!

Thank you. I mean it.

TWENTY-FIVE

Is everyone still there?

As time wore on, we saw less of some friends and acquaintances. Some of it was just because they saw less and less of us – we could no longer socialise outside of our house, so for some people we were out of sight and no longer on their minds. Occasionally a player Brian had coached would visit, and I know it brought Brian happiness but I also saw it brought discomfort for those who had only known him professionally.

Even when I was a little embarrassed at the state of our attire or the house, I never turned away anyone who came to see us. I needed to see people just as much as Brian did.

Loneliness is awful, and it was awful for both of us. Life alone is too quiet, too bleak. A little noise, laughter and conversation was like light coming through a dark window.

I wrote this letter in frustration when Brian was still mobile.

Dear friends and family,

You are all dear to us. I know what wonderful people you are. I know that if I asked you for anything, you would get it for me. You'd pay for it, no questions asked. I know that you are there if I ring for a chat. You ask after Brian. You tell me how much you admire my devotion to him.

I am not being sarcastic: I mean it. I love you.

And I understand why you don't come to see Brian. I know you want to remember the Brian of five years ago. I know it is hard to see him like he is.

But he is lonely, and this is not about you!

He is only awake about six hours a day. They are spent in front of the TV or listening to me in the kitchen. I rarely leave the house – what have I got to talk to him about anymore? It is no life.

He is forgetting, but he does not forget everything.

I think he feels forgotten, though. Where are the people he used to spend time with?

If you come, he will be happy to see you. It will break the boredom for him. It will enhance his life. It will bring him some joy – just for a moment, but it will be real joy. Your presence might spark a memory for him, put a smile on his face.

He is so stoical. He never complains. But he hardly ever smiles anymore – would you?

Those extraordinarily dedicated friends who do come, who sit with him when they can, are also running out of things to tell him. Grant comes up from Canberra, Greg comes every Saturday, and Garry is here every chance he gets.

Please call in. Just once. Many people say to me, 'Is there anything you need? You just need to ask.' Well, I am asking! It is all we need.

This is the letter I wish I could send – but I won't. It sounds angry and selfish. I know that you all have your own lives. It is one of the complications of younger onset dementia. So many of you are still working full-time. Like us, many of you still have children living at home, or there are new grandchildren to play with, elderly parents to care for, long-awaited overseas holidays to take and your own health to look after.

When you ask if there is anything he needs, I will say, 'Just a visit, if you have time.' Some of you will come. Some of you will mean to come. Some of you will tell me you're sorry but you just cannot see him like he is, and I will tell you I understand (I do).

But if you read this now, please remember this: a visit can mean more than you think it will. Even one visit can bring joy. A conversation about a remembered shared experience might give someone something to talk about for days.

I know several couples living with younger onset dementia, and they all say, 'No one comes to the house anymore.'

It is the hardest thing.

TWENTY-SIX

The toughest decision

By the spring of 2014, Brian still looked fit and healthy. He was 58 years old, and he was still very strong. Only his brain was letting him down, and it had begun to put him, and me, in physical danger.

He could no longer fathom the world around him and, as I was his constant companion, I am sure he thought I was somehow conspiring to put him into dangerous situations and trying to hurt him. He felt the need to protect himself from all outside forces and from me.

The only way to take away his fear and anger was chemically. Sedatives have a lot of side effects, especially drowsiness, but they would help to calm his anxiety. A sedative prescribed to Brian by his doctor would keep him and me safe.

It was not what I wanted to do. It was completely outside my promises to Brian and my intentions to assist him to continue fighting his disease. It felt like I was betraying him.

The decision had been coming for weeks, but it still felt sudden and ill-considered. I like to consider all positions when I decide something – I don't like knee-jerk reactions. But as Brian's dementia worsened, I never felt like I had enough time to make any decisions. I had to make them, and I had to make them quickly.

I know that there is a great surge of opinion now against chemically restraining people in nursing homes. I understand that. It is not up to the people who are caring professionally for someone to decide how to make their own lives easier.

My decision was made to make Brian feel easier. He was fearful and defensive. If his disease was cancer and we decided to up the morphine to take away the pain, no one would question the decision. I wanted to take away his fear, and make him feel safe and calm.

I did not want to abandon him just because it had become too hard. He was still my husband and I still wanted him at home. I know he wanted to be at home. I am sure he wanted his home to feel as safe as it always had. I am sure he wanted to no longer feel angry. He was a gentle and kind person; this constant anger was a new thing for him. His fears were imagined, and I needed to make them go away.

Until then, any time I had asked for advice from friends and family it was really to affirm a decision I had already made. I had already decided on my path and just wanted a pat on the back to help me along.

This time, I was guided all the way by experts. This time, I had no choice but to submit to the advice and decisions of his doctor. The only solution was to hospitalise him under his doctor's care until the correct medication was established and then maintained.

I did stand my ground on taking him home, though. I was advised against it, but I know I made the right decision.

When Brian woke on what I now think of as his last 'real' day, he let me take him to the bathroom, but I don't think he knew who I was. I did manage to get him into the shower, but he resisted all my efforts to dress him, pushed me to the wall in the entrance way and tried to punch me.

Liam ran downstairs and calmed him down, dressed him and asked him not to hit me. He was wonderful when dealing with Brian, although it made him very angry and upset.

Brian ate breakfast quite happily, and we got ready to take him to see his geriatrician, Dr Clair Langford, at Bulli Hospital.

He did not want to get into the car, though he seemed okay with going to see Dr Langford – I know he liked her a lot. By the end of our street, he had started trying to get out of the car, and he kicked and swore at the car door all the way to Bulli, about 25 kilometres away. I was so stressed by the time we got there that in the reception area I started to cry. Dr Langford arrived to see me and took me straight into her room without Brian, leaving him in the care of a nurse.

I explained his recent behaviour and told her about my little car accident the week before, when I had rammed the bollard in the car park. She did not want me to put him back into the car, and talked to me about sedating him and putting him into care. We settled on him going by ambulance to Wollongong Hospital under her care for a few days.

I raced home to pick up his things and followed him there.

Because he was sedated, the ambulance trip and the arrival at the geriatric ward of the hospital weren't too bad. But on my arrival I was shocked to see two security guards sitting by his door; Brian had needed to be subdued when his sedation had worn off, until the next dose took hold. In between sedations, he was pretty angry with me.

I told the guards as I walked in that I hoped they had books to read as they would not have anything else to do. They were dubious initially but, by the second day, they agreed with me. I also suggested they remove their uniforms and just wear plain shirts.

That way Brian would not see them as authority figures and think he was in trouble, but would assume they were just two blokes who were helping him.

A patient with dementia who is in care will not behave better because they think they are in trouble – and if they feel they are being punished unjustly, their behaviour will just be worse. They are not children to be disciplined. They are people with a different sense of what is happening to them, and they feel they need to protect themselves from the unknown.

I made the decision on my own to hospitalise Brian and chemically restrain him, but I had wonderful moral support that week.

I arrived at the hospital at 8 am each morning and stayed until 8 pm each evening. It meant I could help the nurses taking him to the bathroom, showering him, changing him and changing the bed.

My wonderful friend Kim delivered coffee to me every afternoon when she finished work. Brian's teammates from his Dapto under-17s rugby league team came in a group to talk to him and allowed me a little time away from his bed.

Grant came and spent a day at the hospital with us. He stayed the night at our house and went back in the morning so Brian would not be alone.

Our siblings and my parents came to help Brian and I pass the time.

He had been so frightened for weeks; now he was calm and sleepy.

The geriatric ward of the hospital is a challenging environment. Not all the patients have illnesses that affect their brain, and it must be terrifying for them to see the frightened people suffering from dementia. The ward can be noisy and often smells bad. The staff are stretched to their limits, and the door to the ward is locked at all times.

It must be dreadful if that is the last place you stay in your life.

My darling husband,

Today has been the hardest day I have experienced in this journey so far.

The final stages of your disease have begun.

I have made some decisions for you. I feel that these are the decisions you would make for yourself.

In order to take away the fears you have experienced over the past few months, you will be medicated to keep you calm and comfortable.

No more horror trips in the car. No more forgetting who I am. No more terror of unknown places.

Just sleepy, quiet times while your body slows down in line with your cognition.

I can see how much you hate having no control over what happens to you. I can see how scared you are. I can see how much this is hurting our boys. I can see that the only solution to this is to keep you in a calm and sleepy state for the rest of your life.

My head knows this is right, but my heart is not in it.

I will bring you home again in a few days, my love, and I will look after you for as long as you need looking after. We will continue to look for the joy in our lives.

I love you, my darling. I am so sorry. This is not what I had planned.

TWENTY-SEVEN

Experts by our side

The palliative care team from Wollongong Hospital are some of the kindest, most professional people I have ever met.

In my initial meeting with Dr Roger Cole, and every time a member of the team came to my house, I felt listened to and supported. I was never judged or delivered a lecture. I was given the chance to do this my way. I hope I had given Brian an opportunity to go to the end of his life in a way that was calm and safe.

Four years later, I saw the wonderful Dr Cole again when my father, after a long stay in hospital, decided to cease his medications and die at home in my mother's gentle care.

Dr Cole remembered Brian and me. He dealt just as beautifully with my parents as he had with us. What a remarkable man. To face people's grief in the face of death every day and make you feel cared for and important is a fantastic skill. I hope all palliative care teams are as good.

Dear Dr Cole,
Meeting a palliative care team is a little confronting. A *lot* confronting, actually.

At the start of our meeting, it did feel a bit like an inquisition. But I realised that your questions not only let you know how I felt, but also made me understand how I felt too.

You explained – with your wonderful, calming demeanour – that Brian could go to a nursing home. He was strong and healthy.

I explained how only his body was healthy. His mind was almost gone, and his body was letting him down by pumping along so nicely.

If he was put in a nursing home, they would not put up with Brian's behaviour. They would sedate him. He would have to wait around when he wet himself until someone had time to change him. I will change him straightaway. If they let him walk around, he would only bang on the door, begging to be let out to go home. I will keep him at home where he wants to be.

He will lie in bed and his body will decline, bringing it in line with his brain.

If he keeps stumbling around, he will fall and could break a bone, suffer pain, and then the same thing will happen: he will be put to bed, sedated.

My way takes away the risk of him suffering that pain.

Dr Cole, you told me people don't do this. They give their partner, parent or child to an institution because it is too hard.

How can it be too hard to look after someone you love?

When Brian was diagnosed, if I had shown him a photo of himself today, he would have looked me in the eye and said, 'Don't let me go there.' I am shortening this journey for him. Today I take control of this bloody disease and get rid of it in the only way possible.

It will be my pleasure to clean, feed and comfort him.

You told me that it will challenge your team to support me in this, but that it is good to challenge them.

Thank you for supporting me. Thank you for telling me I am right.

TWENTY-EIGHT

Welcome visitors

Of course, plans for life never run smoothly. On many occasions I must have looked like a madwoman as I tried to stay on track for the outcome I wanted. Thank god the people I love, and even the professionals, trusted me enough to help me, despite my displays of lunacy.

The day Brian returned home under the care of the palliative care team was also the day my friends Emma Muller and Catherine Pitchford were arriving from New Zealand and England to visit.

Emma and Catherine are sisters. Their father, the late Brian Pitchford, had been the chairman of Warrington Rugby League Club when we arrived there in 1985. The girls and their mother, Carol, had become – and remain wonderful friends – of ours.

Emma had married a New Zealand rugby player and had emigrated to New Zealand. Catherine had decided to move to New Zealand too, and her flights meant she had a couple of days' stopover in Sydney. Emma flew in from Auckland to enjoy a visit with us together. It had been arranged for months. Another friend, Amanda Mackay, was picking them up to deliver them to my house; Amanda's husband, Greg, had passed away the year before. When the arrangements had been originally made, I had no idea of the chaos that day was going to bring.

The morning that Brian was scheduled to arrive home from hospital, I was trying to get the house and room properly organised for him. I took delivery of a huge hoist and sling, ramp and commode at 8.30 am. Our friend Grant was with Brian in the hospital so he would not be alone. Grant expected to be there an hour or so before the ambulance picked Brian up; he had to be in Canberra for an appointment in the early afternoon.

All night I had been going through things in my head for my new job as Nurse Karen McNagalot. In mulling over his medications, I realised there was a discrepancy, so at 10 am I called our new palliative care nurse to sort it out.

I was on the phone, new equipment in the doorway, when Emma and Catherine called out from the door. In my panic, I had completely forgotten they were arriving – even though I had made an emergency dash to the supermarket for supplies for them an hour before. I thought it was my mum or a postie so called out and asked them to wait. Of course, I realised in the next 30 seconds, and then had to finish my call and get them inside. Now the entrance way held all the equipment, suitcases and four hugging friends.

At that moment, the community nurse arrived to do an occupational health and safety check. She did not look impressed! To top it all off, the only part of the emergency supplies I'd bought that was still sitting on the bench was a *big* bottle of gin. I could tell she did not approve of Brian coming here from hospital, and the look on her face was priceless. (Of course, by the time she left, she completely understood.)

We stayed in all day, waiting for Brian to arrive home. Grant had stayed with Brian for at least six hours, and missed his appointment in Canberra. By the time Brian arrived home at 5.30 pm, he was hot and sweaty and looked most uncomfortable.

But my friends took it all in their stride … as only the closest of girlfriends could.

Dear Emma and Catherine,

What a blessing that you arrived this weekend!

You were both wonderful, never batting an eyelid as you helped me roll Brian over, strip him, wash him, change him and dress him. Emma, you talked to him as normal and I even heard him call you by name. He hasn't spoken my name in six months!

I cooked you both an awful dinner and served it two hours later than I had expected to. You waited, pretended it was good and drank champagne. Catherine, your jet lag must have been dreadful by that time, but we stayed up and talked. I really needed that!

I missed you both as you headed out to see the sights on Saturday morning, but I needed the time with the nurses to learn how to use the sling and hoist. I'm so glad you did that. If you had stayed in, I would've panicked about you wasting time here with me. Emma, you are amazing the way you took charge and found shopping centres and local tourist attractions you had only been to once or twice before.

The normality with which you ordered takeaway and ate it with me and Brian was fantastic.

I treasure the photos of us all by his bed. The pictures don't capture how happy Brian was to be fed salt and pepper squid, but we know just how much he enjoyed the little party in his room.

I was sad to say goodbye again when you left on Sunday. It was fantastic to have you here at such a crucial time. I could not have gotten through the weekend without your help and support.

Old friends are the best!

TWENTY-NINE

Quiet house

After that first frantic weekend, our house became quiet and calm, a place where sadness took over from the joy I had wanted to go on experiencing forever.

There were no more impatient voices demanding cooperation. The loudest noise was the music playing constantly during the day in an attempt to help Brian discern between day and night.

Deciding to bring Brian home affected not only me but the boys, too.

Liam lived at home during that time. He worked in Sydney and left home before 5 am each morning to start work at 7 am, avoiding the traffic hold-ups on the way. He worked hard and needed to sleep, but he would be my back-up at night if anything unforeseen happened. I didn't ask him if he was prepared to take on the extra caring assistance roles I might give to him – I just assumed he would.

In the final months of Brian's life, Brett visited when he could. He helped me to roll and clean him if he needed changing when a care worker wasn't available. On one occasion, he was helping me with quite a mess. His job was to help me roll Brian onto his side and gently hold him while I cleaned him up. Brett asked me to hurry up. I told him it was good practice for when he had to do this for me. He mumbled something about putting me into a nursing home!

Dear Liam,

I am so proud of you.

Twice this week you have shown me the man inside you.

Last week, when Dad 'attacked' the new carer, you took charge. Changed him. Washed him. Gave him dinner. Put him to bed and stroked his hand until he slept.

This week, when Dad cornered me and swung to hit me, you wrapped your arms around him. Told him not to hurt me and helped me dress him.

You were tender and loving with him, and he was safe and comfortable with you.

In the hospital that night, you cried. I know you miss your dad. I know you love your dad. I know you want the best outcome for him and agree with my decision to sedate him so I can look after him from now on.

This is so very hard for you to live with.

Thank you for your support of me and to him.

I love you dearly.

THIRTY

Care and dedication

When Brian came home from hospital, the help we needed from care workers had changed. Until then, our care workers had offered respite and assistance with daily needs. Now we needed much more hands-on help, and the carers needed to have more clinical experience. The new care company engaged to assist with Brian's day-to-day care was a small, private, family-owned operation. It was well-run and efficient and I found the vast majority of their workers dedicated and caring. I built a strong rapport with our most regular attendees.

Jacob, the son of the owner, was our most regular helper. He was studying to become a paramedic and his medical knowledge was invaluable at times. Our rapport was so good he would sometimes stay and have dinner after he helped to put Brian to bed in the evenings. I still count him among my friends.

Sally and Pam came often, always smiling and patient, ready with a funny story while helping expertly and efficiently.

One worker never smiled, and always complained about her back. I know she must have been tired – the work is hard – but she was officious and vocal about what she would and would not do. One evening, as we were hoisting Brian into bed with the mechanical lifter, the battery died, leaving a frightened Brian suspended in midair. She just shrugged and said she could not help. I knew it was my fault for not charging the battery, and luckily my neighbour and his son came to our aid and helped me lift Brian safely from the sling to the bed. It's not the way things are supposed to be done, but desperate times call for desperate measures.

Peta was another favourite. She had a large family and most of her children were still of school age. I was always amazed at her happiness and energy. She was a pleasure to have in our home every time she was there.

Dear Peta,

I missed you this morning. You brighten our day.

You are the best worker and most caring carer I have ever met. You get more of a response from Brian than even I do.

Thank you so much for all your help with his showers and changing.

The most important thing you do for him, though, is tease me. He loves it when you promise him I will cook pancakes for breakfast! I am sure he has a crush on you!

Your being here last week while I had two days away gave me the confidence to go – I knew if you were here checking on the respite carers, morning and evening, that nothing could go wrong.

I have never seen anyone so good at their job – you most definitely deserve more money!

Thank you also for being my friend.

THIRTY-ONE

After life

Discussing end-of-life wishes with a partner, even one who has all their cognitive skills, must be very hard. Being given a diagnosis of a terminal illness makes the prospect of dying very real. I know I have spent my life ignoring the inevitable, thinking it would never happen to me. How do you ask someone what their preferences are? *Cremation or burial? Who do you want to speak for you? Do you want to donate your organs?*

After he was diagnosed, Brian became so intent on beating the disease I was not game to discuss what would happen if it killed him. How could I ask him what he wanted to happen to his body after he died? We had never discussed it before, and it just did not feel like the right time to start the discussion.

Early on, we had followed all the advice about getting Enduring Power of Attorney and Guardianship sorted very quickly. As his cognition declined, this did cause Brian some angst. If I bought new clothes for myself, he would tell our friends that I had spent all our money and there was nothing left for him. (Luckily, online banking meant I could quickly show him our account balances to reassure him that was not the case.)

But if I had asked him what he wanted to happen when he passed away, he would have accused me of trying to kill him. He was already frightened. I did not want to frighten him further.

Brian and I were too young to have thought about our deaths and funerals. We had wills – that is just sensible – but they were basic.

We were not really going to die, were we?

Dementia is not the type of terminal diagnosis we ever expected. Its very nature makes it impossible to make decisions about it when you finally realise what is happening.

We had discussed brain donation with Dr Clair Langford, but I have never felt a need to know what caused Brian's dementia. It is what it is. I didn't need to apportion blame. I watched some of our friends struggle with anger over what caused their partner's disease – genetics, mobile phones, work accidents. Some are obsessed by it, wanting to pin down a cause, wanting to sue someone for compensation. It seemed like a waste of energy to me.

I am glad Brian and I did not spend all our last years together trying to work out what went wrong. It has seemed much more important to make every day count, to live the life we still had and to feel happy – not angry or sad.

But, in the last months of Brian's life, I was asked to face a proper diagnosis.

I had cut people off who wanted to ask me about head injuries from rugby league. I was not interested in class actions like they have in the US. Who do we blame if it is from a footy injury, anyway? Brian's parents for registering him to play? A kid who tackled him? The Australian Rugby League itself?

It's just life. It was a life Brian loved. It was so good to us. It paid the bills, meant we easily bought a home, gave us great holidays, gave us the chance to live and work in England. Ultimately, it was because of Brian's rugby league career that we have our beautiful boys; their adoption would never have happened without it.

But ...

Letters for Brian

Dear Brian,

On Monday I had a meeting with Dr Clair Langford. She has been to a conference in Boston where she learned about chronic traumatic encephalopathy (CTE). Football players' dementia. The more she heard, the more she thought how much it fitted your symptoms.

Apparently, you don't need to have been completely knocked out to suffer the repercussions of a hard knock to the head or a jolting tackle. You can have a genetic susceptibility to it occurring. I can only remember two occasions when you were knocked out while playing, and I know you were also knocked unconscious once when you were about 12. I remember how sick you were after your concussions and how confused. Now the researchers believe that just a knock can cause tau protein to grow in the brain. It would certainly explain why your symptoms have been so different to those of others we know with Alzheimer's disease.

We had discussed brain donation with Dr Langford before, but I wasn't that interested. Confirming your diagnosis after you have died seems a bit superfluous and one less brain to test for Alzheimer's disease doesn't sound like it will make much of an impact on the research industry. But Dr Langford talked to me about the fears she knows Narelle holds for herself, and for your nephews. I know you would do anything for your baby sister and her beautiful boys. So now I must make a decision for you about things I don't want to think about.

When you die, I would have to call the researchers, who would collect your body and return it, minus your brain, to a funeral director. Your coffin would have to be closed. It would mean that I would lose your physical being very quickly and that Brett and Liam, your siblings and your friends would never see you.

I did not realise what a big decision this is. It is a hard thing to plan. Thinking about what becomes of your body while you are still alive is very, very hard. I feel like I am wishing you gone – and I am not. Just mulling it over in my head feels wrong, disloyal, like I am murdering you. How am I going to actually talk to anyone else about it? What would *you* do?

I have asked your sisters to come and talk to me. I have no idea how I will broach the subject with them. I doubt I will be able to talk to our boys about it.

End of life sucks.

THIRTY-TWO

A shrinking world

The time at home marched by slowly. The days had a strict routine: care workers, friends, boredom, and lots of time alone in front of the TV and computer.

I struggled with loneliness and gained weight.

I read all I could about adjusting medication, and mitigating the risk of bedsores and urinary tract infections. I tried to cook appetising food that could then be blended to an unappetising puree.

We listened to music and podcasts. I was torn between trying to stimulate Brian's interest in something, anything, and leaving him in peace. I had no way of knowing which he preferred.

Our regular care workers were our friends, visiting for 45 minutes every morning and half an hour every evening to help me shower and change Brian and put him back to bed. They talked to Brian and showed him great respect. I learned from them daily. Rolling, washing and changing Brian was a two-person job. Sometimes there was no other person to help. They taught me tricks to help me do it alone if he needed changing and cleaning when there was no one else. I also had a couple of hours respite a week so I could just get out of the house. A care worker would come and just sit in the house so Brian was not left alone. He wasn't even aware they were there.

My parents called by a few times a week. My brother and sister-in-law came every Saturday: Greg would mow the lawn or sit with Brian while Kaz and I walked or swam to get me out of the house. At least twice a month I saw a friend, or one or both of Brian's sisters, and a couple of really close friends visited a bit more often. Liam was living at home, and Brett came when he could.

Some days, everything just felt flat and uninspiring. Significant days – anniversaries, birthdays – held no significance. I could not find the joy now that was required for any sort of celebration.

On Brian's 59th birthday, I wanted to celebrate, as I expected it to be his last. But I just couldn't muster the energy. I did feed him chocolate with every meal and made salt-and-pepper squid for dinner so that he had some treats in the day, but I just felt too sad. Brian's sisters, Debbie and Narelle, visited and brought ice cream for him – a great present. There are few other gifts that he would have been able to use or would bring a smile to his face.

Facebook, surprisingly, turned out to be a panacea to my sadness. I don't know how many messages Brian received – 40? Messages from old schoolfriends, new friends, English and Welsh rugby league players, friends he would expect to hear from and others that surprised me. Brian was well remembered and well thought of – of course he was. Grant came too, and he brought his daughter Jaslyn with him. Brian opened his eyes wide and smiled when he saw her – it was brief, but he seemed to recognise her.

It was lovely to see him connect with someone. I saw it so little.

The time I spent on my own in the house dragged and I felt isolated. I couldn't even think of things to say to myself.

Dear Brian,

I am pretty sure my brain has stopped functioning properly.

I cannot stay focused on any activity. I can't watch a TV

show without flicking around the channels. I can't finish reading a newspaper article. Books feel beyond me – way too big a commitment! Even a new recipe feels challenging.

I can't think of anything to do on my respite afternoons.

When I do get a chance to swim, I seem to have lost the ability to daydream, as I used to do while I swam. Now I just try to count the laps.

I don't ring anyone because I have nothing to say.

I never guessed I could be at home for a year without seeing many people and stay sane. I was always the gregarious one, needing to find things to do and people to be with.

What can I talk about now? Your medications, your pain level, whether you are eating or not, how the hydrangeas are flowering. Not riveting stuff!

Facebook sometimes feels like an outing, where I can live vicariously through others' lives. I am in contact with people who I haven't seen in 10 and even 20 years. Our friends are constantly travelling, both here and abroad. As soon as one comes home, another one choofs off somewhere. I have followed them to New York, Thailand, Bali, India, Vietnam, Cambodia and Switzerland, on cruises and in campervans. It's how I know the world is still turning.

It's quiet here. I don't say much to you. I do tell you when someone has telephoned, or visited while you were asleep. I tell you I love you. I don't like to remind you of the things we can't do anymore. I feel guilty if I go out. I don't tell you if I have been anywhere – I imagine you would just be wondering why I did not take you with me. But not telling you extends the silence.

My world is shrinking.

THIRTY-THREE

Stay with me

After we brought Brian home from hospital with the guidance of the palliative care team, I went to see Brian's GP to explain what had happened. He kindly offered regular home visits on his way to the office from his nursing home duties, and we discussed general treatment of Brian's health.

I remember distinctly that he said, 'Please don't ask me to prescribe antibiotics for minor infections. There will be no point in treating them.' I assured him we were on the same page. I did not want Brian's new situation to go on and on.

I was of course also in constant touch with Dr Langford and the palliative care team. All were wonderful in assuring me I could call if I needed anything.

At this stage, Brian could not tell me anything about how he was feeling or if he was in any pain. I knew he still heard me and understood my questions, but his responses were often ambiguous and my interpretations could have been wrong. So I had only my own observations to work out if something was wrong.

I would ask him for a smile sometimes and he would give me one. Some of those smiles would reach his eyes and he would look at me, albeit briefly, with love. Sometimes his mouth would just move back to expose his teeth in what appeared to be a grimace – a smile on command. At least I knew he still had some understanding of the world around him, even if the smile did not express happiness.

I observed how uncomfortable he had become. If I did not move his arms and legs and roll him myself, he would remain for hours in the same position that he was put in when returned to bed. He just seemed to seize up and would groan when I moved him. He had to be moved, though – the risk and pain of bedsores is very real.

I talked to the community nurse and his doctors about my observations and asked for help for him. Muscle relaxants seemed like the answer.

Trial and error was the only way of dealing with problems, and the mistakes I made were horrible for him.

Oh my poor darling,

What a tough week this has been for you. I am so sorry I have put you through this discomfort.

I thought something to relax your muscles would make you feel better so we could stretch out your legs and arms. I had no idea that the long list of side effects in the paper that the chemist gave me would affect you so badly.

At first, it seemed that the small dose was just making you a bit sleepier, but that did not seem like it would be a problem. When I moved you to a full dose, again you were sleepy but the biggest problem seemed to be waking you enough to get you to eat. Within a day, though, I could see the problems escalating. You did not wee for eight hours and when I put you to bed I noticed your right foot was hot and red. By the time I called the palliative care team for advice, your foot was a red balloon that I thought would burst!

The after-hours doctor was kind when she came. She was sure you had an infection and gave you antibiotics. I knew she was wrong. I elevated your foot and gave you an anti-inflammatory and you went to sleep. You had urinated by the morning and your foot looked fine.

You were so hard to wake and were eating next to nothing, so I talked to your doctor and we stopped the tablets. I thought that would be the end of it but tonight, after 36 hours off the tablets, your feet are red, hot and swollen. You haven't urinated for more than 14 hours and even after your usual meds you haven't gone to sleep – you must be very uncomfortable.

I spoke to the palliative care nurse, who offered to come out and catheterise you. I don't want to do that. I am scared for you now. If they catheterise you, we will be coping with the discomfort and infections. Gail has told me about Mike's problems with the catheter, and just today Jenny was describing how David had pulled his catheter out, caused bleeding and ended up in hospital. I don't even want to think about it.

All I want is for you to be pain free.

Please sleep comfortably, my darling.

Although I had agreed not to treat any infection Brian might have with antibiotics, I did not have the courage of my convictions.

Dear Brian,

I have written nothing over the past few months. Life just rolls on day by day but tonight you gave me such a fright!

You seem to have a urinary tract infection.

I had discussed with the doctor that we would not give you antibiotics. I was so confident in that decision.

Today you are weeing blood, and I called the after-hours doctor, who prescribed Keflex.

I cannot let you go through the pain that a UTI would put you through. I hope it clears up quickly.

The realisation that I could withhold the antibiotics and hasten your death was frightening. It left me with a hole in my stomach and I started to shake.

Please don't get sick, my love. I really can live like this for the next 30 years. Stay well. Stay with me. I love you and cannot imagine life without you.

THIRTY-FOUR

Our final days

By November 2015, I had become so accustomed to the life we were leading I thought it would just go on forever. But the reality of Brian's impending death had started to become obvious.

He stopped eating even his favourite foods, and I would spend hours trying to tempt him with morsels of different things. But the weight just fell from his already tiny frame. He smiled less and showed signs of pain and discomfort when we moved him. We increased his morphine to make him more comfortable; he just slept more and ate less. I was surprised that he was still with us for Christmas.

On Christmas Day, Brian came outside with the family. I fed him chicken, baked potatoes and gravy, and he really seemed to enjoy it. He was obviously happy to see Garry and even though it exhausted him quickly, I felt happy to see him smile a little.

If I try to remember now how I felt, I know I felt sad but I truly cannot recall feeling panicked. I did not want Brian to leave me, but I wanted the miserable non-life he was living to end. I had no idea if my voice, my touch or even his medications gave him comfort. I just hoped that, like taking sleeping tablets on a long-haul flight, the time felt shorter to him than it actually was.

∽∽

In the last week of Brian's life, a wonderful friend came to visit. Paul, one of the teachers' college group, had run into Grant in Canberra, when Grant had just returned from staying with us, as he did on alternate weekends. Paul lived six months of the year overseas, and the other part of the year travelling between his homes in Canberra and Port Macquarie.

Over the last few years, Paul had sent messages via other friends when they came to visit, saying that essentially he was too sad to see Brian and wanted to remember him as he had been before the dementia took hold. But this time, he wanted to see Brian. He had not seen him for about six years. Grant explained that if he did not see Brian in the next couple of days, he would not be able to see him at all. Grant returned to Dapto with Paul almost immediately.

They arrived the next Saturday. Brian had not eaten for about five days by then; I could barely get water into him. Brett and Liam, Brian's sisters and several other friends were there as well. We played a game of Scattergories around his bed. We pretended that he played too – on my team. My theory was that the last of his hours would be spent hearing his family and friends laughing, not crying, as I knew he was nearing the end of his life.

When Paul arrived, I woke Brian and told him Paul was here. Paul came in through the study door, loudly retelling the story of the day his tooth had been knocked out playing hockey. As he desperately tried to find his tooth in the grass, all Brian could do was roll around on the ground laughing. He called Brian a 'useless bastard', in the way best mates do.

We are told all the time that people with dementia cannot remember things, or people, or events. I suppose that is expected to be especially true in the last days or hours of life.

Yet my weak, starving, medicated, dying husband's face lit up. His eyes followed Paul around the room, and he laughed out loud.

It brought Brian such joy. I know it was hard on Paul, but it brought him joy too.

Brian loved Paul. Paul loved Brian. In that moment, and now, I love Paul for how he handled something so far outside his comfort zone that he had avoided it until the need became desperate. My heart still swells with gratitude.

∽∽

Brian and I had never discussed dying or funerals except as a joke when our boys had asked us what we would do, in the way children do. *Do you want to be buried or cremated? Where do you want your ashes?*

Plan A had been that the ashes of whoever died first would be kept by whoever was still living, and when both of us had died the boys would mix both sets of ashes together and throw us to the wind. We did not make a pact for that; it was just our answer to a question. When Plan A was hatched, we imagined we would be 95 years old when we died.

Now planning for his death felt like a betrayal. I had promised him I would help him to do everything to fight his disease. There was no more fight left in me, and there was no more fight left in him either.

I decided that I could not allow researchers to take Brian's body. If he had been in hospital, I may have thought differently. In a clinical situation, with all the systems in place, I think I could have allowed staff in uniform to wheel him away to another part of the hospital.

Brian, however, was at home. I could not imagine having someone sitting and waiting for him to take his last breath – or, worse, to persuade me while he was still breathing to allow them to remove him from our home.

We had friends stay over for New Year's Eve, and Brian knew

they were there and responded to their presence. For a few days, no amount of my prompting could get him to eat, and the doctor advised me it was dangerous to just keep putting food into his mouth. I made him chocolate drinks and gave him juice, but after five or so days he stopped swallowing those too. I think New Year's Day was the last time he ate. I moistened his mouth with water and a bottle of solution the community nurse gave me.

I did not think he could continue that way for very long, and I let our friends know. I am glad I did that. It meant that many of our friends made sure they came to see him. We had a house full of wonderful people over his last weekend. Friday and Saturday we sat with him, played board games on his bed and told stories to make everyone laugh. My old friend Kim McKeen had delivered coffees to me when he was in hospital and now she turned up with finger food; we made G&Ts and played his favourite music loudly throughout the house. It was a house full of love. Brian's sisters, my family, our boys, Grant, Garry, Paul, Jenny and lots more walked in and out all weekend.

I was frightened that Brian would not know I was just behind him in my bed all night, so I moved his day chair beside his bed and slept in it with my hand on his all night. I did not want him to feel alone even for a moment. Morphine injections kept him comfortable in those last days, too.

When we woke on Sunday, I could tell things had changed. He was not responding in the same way. He was totally exhausted; his mouth was so dry, and the best I could do was to swab his mouth with water and watch him constantly. It was still a noisy house, but I talked softly to him and I so hope he understood my messages of love.

I look back now and realise that the smells from his breath and his body could have been unpleasant, but I was drinking him in. It gave me something more of him to sense. I watched him, taking in every line of his face; I touched him and smelled him to try to keep him in me for as long as I could. I did not want to let him go. I wanted it over for him, but not for me.

Monday morning, 8 am, while I sat holding Brian's hand, his body convulsed and he ceased breathing. Brett and his girlfriend Jasmin were with him too, as was our carer and friend Jacob. The phone rang as this was happening and I saw that it was Garry. Brian stopped breathing for a minute, maybe more. I was crying with Brett but decided to call Garry to tell him straightaway. As I cried down the phone, Brian shuddered and started breathing again. His eyes stared; he was gone, but his heart would not stop. This happened another three times.

I had no idea this could happen. His heart was beating independently of his brain function. Oxygen going in causes a beat.

It was a difficult day, but we all spent time with Brian. Those last days and hours were filled with laughter and happy sounds despite the sadness.

On Tuesday 12 January, at 2 am, Brian stopped breathing. I was in the chair beside him holding his hand.

Our little fox terrier, Dodger, who had sat under Brian's bed for the past few months, refused to cross the threshold into the room. He sat just outside the doorway with his head on his paws.

Brett was upstairs, asleep. I woke him. He came downstairs in tears, kissed his father's head, then sat on the step opposite Brian's bed and waited.

I woke Liam. He asked me to let him sleep. He got up at 4 am and drove to his job in Sydney as usual. It was his way of coping.

I telephoned my brother, Greg, who arrived 20 minutes later with my sister-in-law Kaz.

I called the funeral director.

At 3 am, a beautifully groomed man and woman arrived,

dressed professionally and driving a hearse. They checked Brian's pulse, did some legal paperwork, reverently placed him in a body bag and moved him onto a gurney that they wheeled out to the driveway. I cried with Kaz as I watched my husband leave our home for the last time.

It was the middle of the night but I felt like I needed to tell someone, and I did not want to wake my parents or our friends. So I called one of our old friends, Alan Middleton, in England to let him know, because I knew he would be awake.

Greg tried to get me to go back to bed but I did not want to be alone in 'our' room now that Brian was gone. Greg gave me a pillow and told me to lie on the lounge. I told him I could not sleep. The next thing I knew it was 6 am.

I woke to find that Alan had announced Brian's death on Facebook. I had not told him he couldn't, and I really didn't mind, although I thought it was a funny thing to do (the new modern way?). The news had circulated unbelievably fast and was on a local radio news bulletin in Wollongong by 7 am.

> My darling, I wish you were here.
>
> What a tough couple of weeks we had. I hope that my decisions on your care did not give you pain. You gave no indication that they did – but that might have just been you sucking it up to make me feel okay. I remember we said we would try drugs at the end of our lives because they must be good. We didn't get our silly fantasy of going out at the end together, but I am sure the morphine and midazolam made you feel better. I could see your legs and arms relax a bit from the stiff, contracted positions your muscles had been holding them in.
>
> I know you did not want me to prolong the experiences of this last year for you by killing off the little infections invading your body. If you could have spoken, I am sure you would have said, 'Just shoot me.'

What a cruel system we have for the end of our lives. If you had been a horse in a paddock, the RSPCA would have had me gaoled for leaving you in that state.

It's over now.

You wouldn't believe what a splash you have made on social media. Facebook (I doubt you have ever seen a Facebook page) and Twitter (I cannot explain Twitter – I don't know what it is) went ballistic. There have been tributes to you in all the Australian papers, and in the *Warrington Guardian*; you made it on Prime, WIN, ABC, BBC, Sky, Fox and umpteen radio stations. I have been overwhelmed by the number of people contacting me on the phone, in cards and letters, via SMS, Facebook and email. I had to take the phone off the hook for a while yesterday.

There is no point in crying. You know how much you will be missed. You know how much you were loved. I wanted you to see your family and hear the happiness in this family. This family you created. This family you made so happy. You gave us all so much love.

You were a remarkable man. My remarkable man.

THIRTY-FIVE

How to say goodbye

It is important to plan a funeral. Maybe it is important to plan your own funeral – you want people to get it right.

On the morning Brian died, the first person I called after my parents and Brian's sisters was Garry Posetti. He had had a hell of a week. His partner Jenny's dad had passed away on the same night as Brian, and they were trying to get to Condobolin to be with her family.

When Garry returned, we sat with a mutual acquaintance, Steve Parsons, the celebrant whom I wanted to conduct the funeral.

I had made a list of notes for Steve about Brian. I wanted him portrayed as more than a league player; anyone who wanted to know what Brian had achieved as a coach and player could read his Wikipedia page.

Steve was pleased with the list and said he wished more people would do that. On the day of Brian's funeral he turned my list, almost verbatim, into his eulogy. Not a word of what he said was incorrect. I was so grateful for that.

Among the details about Brian's life, I wrote about his character, and the joy and love he had found in his life.

If Brian warmed to you on your first meeting, you were stuck with him. I don't think he did 'like'; he *loved*.

His closest friends for his whole life were met on his first day in kindergarten and his first day at teachers' college. There were his teammates from minor league, his teammates from the Saints, his teammates from Warrington.

Our boys 'did not come to his world in the usual way' (to paraphrase one of Brian's favourite songs, 'Cat's in the Cradle'). No father loves their sons more than he loved his.

Brian loved simple things. The view of the Illawarra escarpment. Chocolate – the darker and more bitter, the better. My homemade rocky road. Garlic and rosemary potatoes. Spaghetti carbonara. Salt-and-pepper squid from Silver Restaurant at Fairy Meadow. *Fawlty Towers* and *Blackadder*. Long road trips. Museums. History – especially World War I history. Reading thrillers – Robert Ludlum, John Le Carre.

He was an incredibly gentle person who hated fishing because he did not want to see a fish get hurt.

He was gaga for small children and babies (the result of having a baby sister when he was 15).

He was shy.

He was quite happy at home with his family watching TV or playing Scrabble.

He loved to laugh – especially at someone else's expense, and he never took himself seriously. He loved it when someone laughed at him.

He was my brains trust, until I became his.

He taught me that patience, persistence, dedication and unconditional love were the things that made your life work properly. I hope I showed him that I learned those things well.

He was a devoted husband, and I am so proud to have been his wife. I loved him with a great passion.

Looking at this now reminds me how little time a funeral gives you to pay tribute to someone and the life they led.

The announcement of Brian's passing on Facebook brought some unexpected joy.

Brett had set up Facebook pages for both Brian and I long before I explored Facebook or knew what it was. I use my page regularly now. Brian had never used his; I doubt he ever remembered that Brett had shown him that he had one. I posted occasionally on it for him while he was ill.

But Facebook kept people in Brian's life together. There were those Brian had lived near and started school with, who had known Dapto as a country town in the early 1960s. They had all played together and rode bikes around their neighbourhood. Now they are scattered all over Australia and some live in other countries. I suppose because of Brian's rugby league career, they have all remembered him and had followed his career.

On the day Brian died, these people he went to school with and others from his parents' neighbourhood began a conversation on Facebook, and posted memories of him as a boy. I felt like I was eavesdropping, but it was lovely to see names I remembered from school and even people I did not know but who I remembered Brian mentioning over the years. They all had memories of him that were older than my memories of him.

It brought me so much joy. I read them all day and into the night.

I used snippets of those conversations in the program for Brian's funeral, asking their permission and even having a long conversation with a couple of them. Even 24 hours after Brian had died, I was able to find some joy. I know from the comments of his childhood mates that it bought them joy too.

Dear Brian,

I was given some very good advice by a community nurse a week before you died. It did not feel like good advice at the time and was unnerving.

She told me that you would not live for very much longer and that I should make contact with a funeral director.

Initially I was horrified. How do you contact a funeral director for a living, breathing husband?

She had explained that if I waited until after you died, I would be too distraught to be able to answer questions, like your date of birth. She also told me that without a funeral director contact, your body would be taken to the morgue and then you would need to be shifted again to a funeral home. She talked about costs, but I did not care about the costs. She also said that a rushed funeral would not be a fitting ceremony and that I needed to think about what you would really like.

I called Amanda Mackay to ask for her advice. I so wish that she had not had the experience to be able to give me advice. She told me that she regretted that she and Greg had never spoken about funeral planning. She also said she could not even remember Greg's date of birth after he died, and couldn't answer even the simplest questions the funeral director had asked. Her dad and her son Kane had to answer for her.

I asked your sisters; they thought it was wise advice. I asked Garry; he concurred.

I still felt wrong about it, but I eventually called the funeral home.

I was so glad you were asleep with the funeral director came. I felt like a criminal. I answered all the questions and was relieved when it was over.

I started to think of music for the funeral. I chose Billy Joel's 'Lullabye (Goodnight, My Angel)' to play when you were carried to the hearse. I cannot remember all the songs I chose but they were all aching love songs. I planned what had to be said. I thought about the anger I would relay about dementia, the sadness I would speak of with you gone, the unjustness of it all. I thought about the photos of us together that I would display. The stories of our life together.

Amanda gave me some more wonderful advice. 'The funeral is about Brian,' she said. 'It is not about you.'

If I had not had those extra days to think about how to celebrate the wonderful life you had led, then you would have had the saddest funeral ever! As it was, I think what we organised for you was a happy and fitting celebration of your life.

I do not regret calling the funeral home early. It was the right thing to do.

THIRTY-SIX

The send-off

Landing at the business end of a funeral was a new experience for me – and what a business it is! Brett, my brother Greg, and Brian's sisters Debbie and Narelle attended the funeral director's office with me to make the arrangements. The funeral director was wonderful. He was kind and empathetic, very well suited to his role.

I was not worried about the cost of the funeral. I knew I did not want it to be extravagant, but I was quite resigned to the fact that it would not be cheap – I did not want to go for the budget option. But I did not expect the 'Do you want fries with that?' upselling that was involved.

In reverence to the St George rugby league colours, Brett and I decided a white coffin with red roses would display Brian's allegiance to the club without actually having to say anything about it. The flower options began at $100, and it was not until afterwards I realised that a basket of chocolates and rocky road would have been much more appropriate for him – Brian would have loved that, and everyone could have taken them home afterwards.

The funeral director asked how I was getting to the service. I said I would drive. My brother was horrified. Apparently, widows cannot drive. The director asked if I would like them to pick me up. I thanked him and said yes. He said that would be $500. Five hundred dollars for an eight-kilometre trip? No bloody way! Brian would be very upset if I spent that much.

I told the funeral director that I would be putting that $500 on the bar at the wake. Greg said he would drive me.

There were restrictions on the type of video file that the photo montage could be uploaded to. Luckily, Brett's beautiful girlfriend Jasmin had connections in the local film industry, and she took on that role. It was very stressful and emotional for her, and I regretted allowing her to do it. She did a beautiful job, but she cried the whole time as she loaded pictures of Brian onto her computer. (I still cannot understand why the funeral home could not just use a CD, or files from a USB – unless it was to sell me something else.)

Choosing the music was equally stressful. Finding a balance that would not create nonstop tears in the congregation was hard. I wanted to have people listen to Brian's favourites – but it turned out he was very fond of dirges, sad folk songs and aching love songs. We ended up playing more upbeat songs from his favourite artists. I still use that playlist sometimes in my car. I think of it as Brian's soundtrack.

On the day of the funeral, I did not know how to conduct myself. I was not sure if I had to be seen as the grieving widow who could not stop crying or if I was the hostess of some sort of party. It worried me a lot as I did not want to 'misbehave'. In the end, I just ran on a full tank of adrenaline and a tin of Rescue Remedy lollies. I just let the day take its course.

About 500 people attended the funeral, and I was contacted by what seems to have been a further 500 people who could not attend but would have liked to.

He was certainly held in high regard.

Liam did not want to attend Brian's funeral. He got up at 4 am and was at work in Sydney at 6 am. His boss approached him at lunchtime to suggest they go together to the funeral, assuring him that I would not care if he came in dirty work clothes. Liam declined. I did not push him to come. If he comes to me one day with regret for not coming to the funeral, I have a DVD of the whole thing that I can still share with him. He is still not ready to watch it.

Some beautiful eulogies were written for Brian from his friends. Some were read at the funeral; others were messages from friends who put their thoughts down on paper.

I knew I could not have talked directly about Brian on the day, or I would have broken down. So I let the celebrant do the formal funeral thing and he said what I wanted to relate to the crowd.

Instead, on the day I stood with his mates and told a story that Brian loved to tell. Garry, Grant, Doug Hearne and John Jansen had told stories, and I felt that with them beside me I could tell a story too.

> I have so many Brian stories, but I cannot tell them to you – way too personal!
>
> Anyone who ever had a conversation with Brian about overseas holidays will have heard this story. I was there when it happened, and I have heard it a million times. He loved to tell it and I thought I'd give it one more airing.
>
> We boarded the cable car that starts in Stechelberg in Switzerland to travel to the top of the Schilthorn. It is the cable car in the James Bond movie *On Her Majesty's Secret Service.*
>
> There are stops on the way up in the villages of Grindelwald and Mürren, and we hoped to spend all day exploring each village on our way to the summit but did not know if we could do that on our ticket. So Brian went to ask the cable car driver.
>
> Brian said, 'Excuse me, do you speak English?' and the driver gave him an emphatic '*No.*' So Brian turned back to me.

A helpful man piped up and said, 'I speak English, can I help you?'

Brian said, 'Thanks, mate, we just want to know if when we get to the next stop can we get out and walk around for an hour or so and catch another car to the next level on this ticket.'

'No problem, I'll ask him for you,' replied the man in a nice Canadian accent.

He turned to the driver and he asked … very … slowly … and … very … loudly in English exactly as Brian has requested. The driver seemed to be listening intently and then he nodded his head.

The Canadian turned back to us and translated: 'He said yes.' He had no idea what he had done. He only spoke English, the same as us.

Brian might have been incredibly rude to his most loved mates, but he would never hurt the feelings of a stranger. He said thanks to the Canadian and then I don't think he could have taken another breath until we got to the next stop five minutes away so he could laugh – a real belly laugh that almost had him on his knees.

He continued to laugh out loud every time he thought of it for the rest of the trip, and he spent the next four weeks listening for tourists asking locals, 'Do you speak English?' so he could give someone the same experience.

Peter O'Sullivan, Brian's colleague at the Dragons and later his assistant coach at the AIS, wrote beautifully of Brian's teaching and mentoring, which were so much more than rugby league skills:

> Brian made a profound effect on thousands of men and young men's lives. He opened avenues for hundreds of young men and created a program from the elite of our game who are littered through the NRL to players from remote parts of Australia who, except for his vision and passion, would never have been afforded this opportunity.

> This is one story that will remain in my memory forever. It was in France at The Somme, one of his favourite places in the world – other than Bolton Abbey or Conwy Castle. One of his great initiatives was to personalise the experience and get the players to research someone from their hometown who had died during the war and find their burial site. I have since been told it was Karen's idea which, like all good husbands, Brian put into action. What an amazing idea to blend a trip to a graveyard into a history and humanity lesson.
>
> One young lad – Pat McPherson from the tablelands in Far North Queensland – his grandfather had died in the war so he set out to find the grave without success. The bus driver took the group to another site close by as a last resort. They quickly he found his grandfather's grave and within a minute he was surrounded by staff and players. In the silence, one of the boys began to sing 'Waltzing Matilda', arm in arm.
>
> To this day, this personifies Johnno's four loves of family, footy, travel and history all rolled into one. What a remarkable impact he had on hundreds of young men who I'm sure didn't appreciate at the time the opportunity to travel, international competition and to open their eyes to parts of the world they could have only previously imagined.

Brett was great support to me on the day. He was the final speaker and spoke beautifully from his heart about his dad.

> There is a moment in everyone's life when you realise the heroes that you look up to aren't invincible. You're born looking up, listening and learning from legendary men and women with all the wisdom of the world, and as you grow you eventually find yourself looking at them eye to eye, comparing yourself to them, and you realise that they taught you everything you know. They made you the person you are. (and eventually they will go).
>
> My father Brian Johnson made me the man I am today. He taught me so much about compassion, mateship, loyalty, perseverance, love, happiness; how sharing is good but chocolate

is better; how you should always fart in the toilet; to always look on the bright side of life; that you'll catch more flies with honey than vinegar; that you are the company you keep; that you can achieve what you want in life if you work hard at it. A lifetime of lessons, lessons I'll pass on to my own.

I've tried to live my life by these lessons and I've tried to be as good a man as my father was. So far I've fallen short but in all fairness Dad left me a nearly impossible task.

He was a legend, he was a superhero, the kind of man that if your feet were cold he'd give you his socks, so you had two pairs and he had none. That's the kind of person he was. He was the most brilliant man I'll ever know and it's horrendous that such a man had to go in such a way. But we won't remember him like that. We will remember him for the person he was and the amazing life that he carved out for himself. He will live forever in our memory of him, in the stories that we tell.

There is a lot of people here today and I thank you, and each one I'm sure has a story about my dad: Brian, Johnno, etc. You might remember him as a brilliant football player, or a young genius, as a devoted friend, or a daggy practical joker who would torment you any chance he got. But for Liam and I, he will always be remembered as Dad.

I remember him walking across glacial waters, in footy shorts and bare feet, just to fetch me a lump of ice to look at. I remember holding onto his back while he swam underwater and it took all of my strength just to hold on. I remember him building us a snowman in the backyard by himself so we could see it from the window; we wanted a snowman but didn't want to go outside in the cold. Gin rummy before bed, chocolate-coated anything, castles, James Bond movies.

He used to make up and sing daggy songs about whatever he was doing at the time – being tone deaf never held him back. For a man who couldn't, he loved to sing – didn't matter if he didn't know the words, or the melody. His little songs were always going on in the background and in time I ignored them, they become just a part of my environment ... until they weren't sung anymore. Then you really miss them, and you can remember every single one of them.

One of my earliest memories of Dad and I together was driving around Stockton Heath, just the two of us, and he taught me the song 'Always Look on the Bright Side of Life'. We were taking turns making up the verses and then both joining in on the chorus, or that's what I thought we were doing …

I want to thank you all so much for being here to say goodbye to my father, and if you can, I think the best way to send him off would be with one of his daggy songs … the very fitting 'Always Look on the Bright Side of Life' from *Life of Brian*.

Brett then led the crowd in an a cappella version of the song. It was fitting and joyous and sad and loving.

Brian was carried from the service to the hearse by his three closest mates and three of his family. I followed directly behind. I stood behind the hearse and did not know where to go from there. The funeral director stood with me. Silently. I spoke to him through gritted teeth: 'What do I do now?'

No one tells you the rules. I hate breaking rules. It is only now as I look back that I realise there are none.

I would put one rule in place, though – don't put up a Facebook post up from a wake. A lady who Brian did not know thought she was at a party with rugby league memorabilia and excitedly shared the day with her friends. My rule: a little decorum is required at wakes.

Dear Brian,

I was so proud to listen to your wonderful friends and our beautiful son talk about you today, and remember all your wonderful achievements and qualities. The photos we displayed showed you as child, as my husband, as a father, a friend, a student, a rugby league player, a teacher, a coach and a traveller. The stories told were funny, touching and at times irreverent.

The music was just your favourites. We carried you out to 'Wish Me Luck as You Wave Me Goodbye'. Upbeat and fitting.

I am proud of the send-off we gave you. I think you would have enjoyed it.

We wasted no words on God. It was a celebration of You. A deserved celebration of a wonderful man.

THIRTY-SEVEN

To Garry

I was, and still am, more than grateful for Brian's best friend, Garry Posetti.

Sometime after Brian's funeral, I told him about the letter journal that I had kept intermittently while I looked after Brian. I told him that I had written a letter to him. He asked to see it and I reluctantly emailed it to him. I knew it would be emotional for him. He said that, after he read it, he had to leave his office and take some time to compose himself in the car park.

We haven't spoken about it again.

Dear Garry,

I don't know why it has taken me so long to write this to you. I guess it is because you have been there all the way along this journey, and before it, and even now after it. I am ashamed to say I take you for granted. Not completely for granted. Your kindness knocks my socks off every time, but the love you have for Brian and I are just there – have always been there. You truly have been our rock.

You, before anyone else, noticed the changes in Brian. You worried about the changes, and you pointed them out to me.

I had been travelling along quite nicely, noticing little things that Brian did – or, rather, did not do – but I was willing to accept the changes. I sometimes told him he was getting just like his dad, but I wasn't too worried about that; I loved his dad. He seemed to be slowing down at work, but I thought he had been doing it for so long that he was a bit bored. He would lose things, or he would tell me that his printer was broken again and I just found his things or purchased a (yet another) printer. He was always so busy, working in the evenings, driving to and from Canberra, studying, travelling to games. I wasn't surprised he was tired and forgetful. But you were.

You and he took our youngest boys skiing. When you came back you called me and asked me out for coffee and a chat. We started discussing his forgetfulness: leaving his keys at a restaurant, losing his ski gloves twice before he got to the car, forgetting to put his gear in the car. I remember laughing because I had been noticing how 'hopeless' he was becoming too but you put it into context for me. By the time we finished coffee, we were both in tears. My acceptance of his eccentricities had been lazy. I just loved him and didn't mind if he changed as he got older.

Suddenly I could see a real problem.

I knew he had been concerned that his cholesterol medication was messing with his memory and that the doctor had taken him off it after being on it about 10 years. I thought that would fix everything. How wrong I was.

Brian did not want me to tell anyone at all once he had received his diagnosis. He tried to hide it from everyone at work, in the family and all our friends. When I needed to talk, it was you I could talk to. When he was ready to talk, it was you he turned to too.

No matter how difficult it became, you always made sure we still went out. Every dinner, show, ski trip, concert – you always included us. You were never embarrassed by his peculiar behaviour in a restaurant. You were attentive and kind to him. You 'Brian-sat' so Jenny and I could go out together.

You tolerated long car journeys with him. You kept him safe on stairs, in cars, on boats. You never treated him like he was a child. His arm jerked one night as you sat next to him and handed him a glass of port. He threw it all over you. He didn't mean to do that. You laughed and you made him laugh.

You rearranged your life in the last year that he worked so you could travel with him to England and France. I know you wanted to go on that trip but mainly you wanted him to be able to go again. You put up with him being awake and trying to get dressed at 4 am – in someone else's clothes. You helped him choose presents for me to bring home. You protected him from what really was workplace abuse from some of his colleagues. You turned those challenges into funny stories to share with him.

When we could no longer leave the house, you brought takeaways here. You sat with him and told him funny stories of your antics at teachers' college and made him laugh. If I told him you were coming over he would start looking for you, wandering around the back garden and calling out your name. (I had to stop telling him in advance of your visits). You took him on golf days long after he could be trusted to hold a club and made sure he would not wander off.

In this last year, you were here or on the phone every day. You sat by him and stroked his arm. You made him smile when no one else could.

You were here at the end, even when seeing him so thin, his skin waxen, his eyes staring, must have been more distressing than you could have imagined.

You held my hand through funeral arrangements. I couldn't have done what I did without you.

You stood at his funeral and spoke of him with love and gave an outline of the real Brian who you knew so well. You led our friends to do the same. You carried him to his last trip in the car.

You put aside your marriage breakdown, your mum's illness, your work, to help look after him. Your grief must be as strong as mine because I know your love for him, in your way, was as strong as mine. No two men could ever have been closer.

You are truly his brother. And mine. I love you. Brian loved you with all his heart.

I don't know a better man than you, Garry Posetti.

THIRTY-EIGHT

You are not with me

My darling husband,

It is four weeks since you died. I miss you so much. It is time to reflect a little in writing. I have been reflecting a lot lately, in my head.

I cannot remember the last time I wrote in this. Certainly it has been months. The last months of your life just became too hard for me to put my thoughts onto paper. I lived through the days, and at night I just tried to sleep and blot it out. I was too sad to make myself even sadder by thinking things through. I am not sure I can do it now.

Recently, the light in your office started switching off for no reason. A faulty wire? It gave me comfort to think of it as a sign and talk, out loud, to you. Whatever caused the light to go out cured itself after a while, and I was disappointed that you appeared to no longer be, in spirit, in that room.

My life stretches before me with a huge hole in it where you should be.

Come back, my darling, and solve all this loneliness. Please?

You made me promise to always be happy. I can be happy about some things. But I will be sad forever that you are not with me.

Epilogue

November 2024

Dear Brian,

It is now nine years since your suffering ceased.

Such a lot has happened in that time. Maybe you know everything and have been watching over me.

At first, I looked for signs of you everywhere – and I found them. Even now I play a silly game when car registration numbers have the letters 'B J' on them, and I try to work out what you might be telling me with the numbers and letters in the rest of the plate. 'BJ 56 OK' would mean it was definitely you talking to me, as it has your initials and birth year. 'OK' would answer any question I was feeling inclined to ask of you. Dumb, eh?! Comforting sometimes, though.

One evening, as I drove the car into the garage, a tawny frogmouth was sitting on our front tap. I had never seen one in our garden before. I expected it to be gone when I walked out of the garage, but it just sat there, looking at me. I had a quick conversation with it and warned it about the cat from the house down the road. The next night, it (was it the same one?) sat on our barbecue and stared into the kitchen at me. I, of course, named it Brian and asked it (you) if it would come every night. It did visit for one more night.

I wondered about transubstantiation. A friend had told me that it was the belief that we all come back as birds. Apparently, that is not the meaning at all. It is a real word though. I am not religious and not Catholic, so I did not know it was to do with the eucharist. So I hung onto the hope that you were a lovely bird for weeks.

The existentialist side of me believes when you are dead, you are gone. I don't really believe you are in the house or a bird. I do believe that I know you so well that in my own mind I carry you as my brains trust and when I need a second opinion, I can formulate what your opinion would be. I ask your opinion on everything important. I ask you about the trivial too – I just knew you wanted me to buy those ruby earrings for what would have been our 40th wedding anniversary.

About five weeks after your funeral, I booked myself on a group walking holiday along the Great Ocean Walk. I was not the most experienced hiker in the group, but I found myself leading the group each day. It was invigorating and I was blessed to be among a group of lovely ladies, all around the same age as me, who knew nothing of my life. I returned still sad but refreshed.

It has spurred on my love of walking, and I bushwalk every chance I get. I am fitter now than I was 20 years ago.

I went back to work to discover that although I worked with wonderful people in a wonderful organisation, the one difficult person in the office made me feel intimidated and bullied. No problem, really. Life is too short to put up with that shit every day, so I left again. It was time to change my life.

I worked for almost two years in community care and loved it. I got to work with the wonderful Jacob and his colleagues, who enriched our lives so much in that last year we were still together. No job had ever felt so satisfying. I tried hard to emulate the very best carers we had had in our home. At almost 60 years old, though, I found it exhausting work with low pay and long hours. In my last week there I worked 65 hours.

A little later, Garry asked me to come and work for him, just three days a week. I moved into furniture retail and have been there for more than two years. I like the routine, chatting to customers and leaving the work behind when I leave at 5 pm. It is almost stressless for me. I like spending 20 or so hours a week with Garry. I am never lonely when I am working.

For a while, I was lucky to have the company of an old friend of ours who had lost his wife ten years before I lost you. We spent some time together kayaking, fishing, skiing, listening to music, and squabbling over our very different political views and religious beliefs. We filled in some time, and we laughed a lot. But I was lonely. Maybe I was even a bit vulnerable at that stage. It was a nice friendship but not a relationship.

The very best advice I was given after your funeral was never to say no to an offer of an event or opportunity. At the beginning of my new, single life I accepted invitations to outings that did not interest me at all but, each time, by the time I got home I would feel much better.

My most reluctant 'yes' was to join a group of ladies to learn to play the ukulele. I thought it a ridiculous idea. Almost nine years later I own five ukes, play in a band and must be held back sometimes from singing solo. The 'Strum Sistas' – Jill, Lois, Melinda and Sharon – are four of the most important people in my life. I never really needed close girlfriends when I had you, but now the 'Sistas' – along with my hiking and skiing buddy Kate, and Kim and Amanda – help me with everything. They are like having a cheer squad.

I went to Italy and Switzerland with our closest friends for Garry's 60th birthday. Sixteen of us stayed in a beautiful villa on the shores of Lake Como. At the end of an amazing week, four of us travelled to Lauterbrunnen, your favourite place in the world. We rented the same flat you and I had rented in 2012 and I played tour guide on mountain walks you and I had done many times over 30 years. It was a pilgrimage for me. You would have loved it.

You were the only thing missing on that trip. Everyone felt it. Your name was mentioned in every conversation. I laughed a lot on that trip, but I cried a bit too.

It is only because of your tutelage that I can now confidently travel alone. I can do it without fear, but I do not find joy in looking at a view alone. I want to be able to turn to someone beside me just to say, 'How good is this?'

I have taken to skiing with gusto and gone from the timid and poorly coordinated skier you knew to a skier who is not quite so scared and can stay upright for most of the day – a huge improvement for such a motor moron! Thank you for joining the ski club and leaving me the membership. It is one of the best gifts I have received.

I know I have your permission to look for love. You made me promise to be happy after you were gone. Many times you tried to talk to me about finding someone else. It was never a conversation I could have with you. We promised we would be together until death, and we did not part until death, so I could never entertain the idea of another man when you were with me. Even as you lay silent and immobile in your bed, I was your wife. Until death.

You secretly made Garry promise that he would look after me and ensure that I married again. When he told me what you'd said, I explained that I thought you were telling him that *he* had to marry me. He was aghast! 'That'll never happen,' he said, and shuddered. (So did I!)

I resisted the prodding from one younger friend to try internet dating sites. I told her repeatedly that I would rather meet someone at a bus stop than by looking at fake pictures and bylines. She finally persuaded me, after a bottle of champagne and two espresso martinis, that any man I might be interested in wasn't sitting somewhere waiting to meet me. He was watching TV, feeling lonely and wishing his wife was still alive. She convinced me that his kids would have put him on a dating site using the same argument. So, if I wasn't there, I would miss my chance.

It has made for some nice conversations with some nice men. Oh, and one scary one! I have had to explain that I don't have an 'ex', I have a 'late' husband. Being widowed has a couple of advantages: I don't carry any anger about my past, and I didn't have to split the proceeds of the last 40 years. (I don't recommend it, though.) Mostly dating is fun. I think that is the point of dating. At times I feel like a teenager. I put on my grown-up look, though, and hope no one notices.

My 'big brothers', Garry and Grant in particular, take their role very seriously and vet any men that come into my life. I did have to tell them to butt out once, though I love that they try to take care of me.

You and I both know I don't do well on my own. I am definitely made to partner with someone else. I like to look after people. I like to cook for someone. I like to share a view. I like to share a bed. I like a bit of attention. I don't think I need to apologise for that. It stops me from feeling so lonely. Sometimes.

I did think I had found someone pretty special, but I was wrong. That's okay. I might try again. You set the bar too high!

Brett met and married the love of his life. You'd love Danielle. She is kind and beautiful. She also loves eating cheese, drinking champagne and buying shoes, and she knows the words to all of Sam Cooke's songs (remind you of anyone?). I did warn Brett that he had found a wife the same as his mum. He said that was okay. Their wedding was beautiful. They were married on Mount Kembla, just down the road from your beloved grandmother's house. The surroundings were so familiar that it felt like you were there too.

As Danni's 'something blue' I gave her the lovely sapphire ring you bought for me in Thailand, for no particular reason, in 1980. I always saw that as a love token so I passed it on to her to symbolise the love you would have shown to her as she entered our family.

You would be so proud of Brett. He is a wonderful husband – he had a wonderful role model.

He has given up his acting aspirations and now works in a care home with vulnerable children. He has always been kind and caring, and he seems to have found a vocation. He is proud of the work he does. I am proud of him.

He is still a musician – that will never stop for him.

Liam still struggles with the loss of the one person who 'got' him. You were his best mate. He suffers without you more, I think, than even I do. He is only just coming to terms with his grief now. He recently started receiving some counselling and I can now see a much healthier young man. I coddled him along during the first five years, which didn't support him to become his own man. I saw a counsellor to talk through trying 'tough love' on him, then threw him in the deep end and made him move from home.

Liam didn't have an easy ride. He got into trouble, slept for a while in his car, lived in a filthy share house with people he hated, and was out of work for a short period. It was hard to watch. Possibly harder than watching you die – that was inevitable.

It took time, and I still supported him – with love and, at times, money – but the outcome has been sensational. He is much happier and now lives independently. He has a job he loves, his only vice is tobacco and he is in a relationship. He visits me regularly for dinner together and never leaves the house without saying, 'Bye Mum, love ya.' I am so proud of how he has turned his life around.

I sold our beautiful house. It was a huge challenge to let go of so many things we made and bought together. I downsized to a townhouse that I am sure we would have been happy to live in together. After four years it is only just starting to feel like a home. Your picture is on my walls and in my heart.

This last year I have spent three months in England, staying between Brett and Danni, who live in the south, and old friends in the north. The trip included a 12-day hike across Yorkshire. I remember you telling me on a drive to Leeds that one day you would walk over the Pennines, so I did it for you. I know you wanted to also do the Pyrenees. That might be a bit too much for me now – but I have it on the list.

I had what so few people get: a great love, and a blissfully happy marriage.

I have only wonderful memories.

I will carry you within me, always.

I will miss you forever, my darling, but my life is not over.

I do hope I am wrong about 'dead and gone'. I want so much to see you again.

From Brian

A true story from Brian's childhood

When Brian died, and his old friends began sharing stories about him on Facebook, I mentioned that I had a copy of a story Brian had written at university as part of an assignment called 'A Chapter from My Autobiography'. It was requested by the Facebook friends and I emailed it to quite a few of them. They confirmed its truth.

Brian was a clever storyteller, and this essay always made me laugh. I had even used it once as a bedtime story for our boys.

A chapter from my autobiography
Brian Johnson

Life as a child was easy. Thinking back it's hard to imagine anything could be so trouble free. That's not to say that I was never in trouble, far from it, but worries were few and responsibilities insignificant. Every waking moment was spent in the pursuit of enjoyment. I found, and still find, life easy to enjoy, easy to live.

Dapto, my home town, at the time of my childhood, was little more than a small rural centre. The surrounding countryside and abundance of friends gave ample opportunities for play. Endless hours of fun were spent hiking around the paspalum and lantana covered hills and plains that started only a stone's throw from my parents' home.

The large area of bushland surrounding Dapto was considered as our own land and we would explore it rigorously. Of course, nearly every other group of childhood explorers thought of it as theirs, but that was of little consequence. We knew it was ours and we explored and named it as we saw fit.

Before continuing, perhaps I should explain who 'we' were. It is only obvious that for exploration you need more than one person. The dangers of 'the bush' were many and only the bravest or most foolish of people would set about exploring it by themselves. Our group was a select bunch which consisted at this early age of about half a dozen members. The only criteria for membership to this group was that you lived nearby (so that our exploratory journeys could be arranged with a minimum of fuss) and we all lived within shouting distance of each other.

There was quite an age range in the group. The oldest, Stephen, was probably nearly a teenager. His greatest claim to fame at this early age was the metal plate he had had inserted in his skull a few years previously. Steve was an adventuresome, athletic sort of person but I guess playing Zorro with a friend on the roof of his house was just too great a test for his agility. When his friend, the would-be bad guy of the Zorro game, lunged forward with his sword, Stephen (or Daddy Long Legs, as he was called) nimbly parried the blow and took a couple of steps backwards to prepare a counterattack. Unfortunately, when he took his two steps back, he was only one step from the edge of the roof, and as a result he crashed headfirst to the ground. That was the sort of person Steve was, always thinking.

My next-door neighbour Rick and I always found the story of Steve's attempt at being Zorro amusing. We would often tell it to each other when we couldn't think of anything else to laugh about. And of course, we often incurred Steve's wrath for teasing him about it. Not that Rick had the right to laugh at anyone. He could do more stupid things in a week than almost anyone else could do in a lifetime.

Rick was the best spitter in the group, which gained him a great deal of respect, for we were at an age where spitting was deemed a mark of manhood. Not distance wise, because he couldn't spit all that far. The amazing part of Rick's spit was the size and texture of each spit, or 'hack', as they were called. He was, I'm sure, suffering from a constant respiratory complaint. That's the only way that it would be possible to spit the way he did. He would spend minutes coughing, groaning and making foul, primitive sounds in order to bring the phlegm up from the lower reaches of his throat, and sucking back the thick green mucus of his nasal passages into his mouth. There, in his mouth, the two would join and mix into the most repulsive porridge-like substance you could ever imagine. When he spat, the greeny-yellow mucus mass would spin lazily in the air. Occasionally a 'lumpier' bit would try to break away from the main section, but it would only get so far before the springy, lifelike mucus would halt its progress and return it to its rightful position within the mass.

Each day on the way to school we would pass the same paling fence. On each consecutive day Rick would 'hack' on the next paling until the whole fence was soon decorated with the dried-out remnants of the contents of his throat. The spit would land in some amazing patterns and the sun would quickly dry it up, leaving silver (if not somewhat lumpy) patterns that would shine brightly when the sun was at the right angle. Even to this day I can imagine nothing that was as repulsive but at the same time as compelling viewing as Rick spitting.

For some reason, Rick's spitting would always have a strange effect on another of our group, Eric. Eric would start laughing from the moment Rick began his strange ritual at the fence. When Rick's spitting was finished, Eric would closely examine the clinging mass, pointing out the different colours, shapes and textures. All the time he'd be laughing, and the laughing would get louder and louder.

Eric was a funny-looking character at the best of times, with bright-red hair, freckles and the biggest set of buck teeth you could ever wish to see. When he was laughing, however, his features would exaggerate themselves so that his teeth would protrude even further, his hair seemed to get redder and brighter, and his freckles would expand to cover his face. Eventually his laughing would take control of him and, falling to the ground, he would roll stupidly, teeth glinting in the morning sun.

Adding Steve, Rick and Eric along with Marc, who as an infant strangled all my mum's chickens, ensured my brother and myself, who completed the group, a very educational childhood. Marc certainly was a strange one. Perhaps it was his premature birth, brought about by a stray cracker that exploded near his mother on cracker night, that affected him. Whatever the reason, Marc had a mania for throwing stones and would throw them at anything or anyone, whenever the mood took him.

As a child it was these people, apart from my parents, that influenced me most; a near-teenager who had a metal plate in his head, the world's foulest spitter, a buck-toothed character who could laugh himself sick, and a boy who loved throwing stones and used to pass his time by strangling chickens. It is no wonder that I developed into the rational, level-headed person that I am today.

As I mentioned earlier, we spent much of our free time exploring the nearby countryside. One of the favourite trips was down to Lake Illawarra. This four-mile journey was a full day's work and required much forethought and planning. A route had to be decided upon, provisions packed and weapons (such as long sticks, and stones for Marc) made ready for use. Weapons were a necessary part of our equipment as it was not unusual to be chased by some farmer's mad dog or the odd silly magpie or plover. We also had to keep a watchful eye for bunyips at Deadman's Creek (which we so named because of all the cow bones that littered the nearby area). Luckily, however, these bunyips, which were known to exist at the creek, never troubled us.

As I grew, so did Dapto. Large housing estates quickly eroded much of the area that we once considered ours. Fortunately, children are adaptable creatures and we soon found sources of amusement in the houses that were being built. The building frames were ideal for climbing and by constant practice we were soon able to scamper expertly through the half-built shells of houses. Chasings was the popular game of the time, and when I think of how quickly and recklessly we chased each other around the narrow beams and rafters, I marvel that any of us ever reached our teens, let alone adulthood.

The building estates also provided us with an excellent way of raising money. By working our way through the houses after the workmen had knocked off for the day, we could collect a small fortune in returnable soft-drink bottles. In one afternoon's work we collected 2 dollars and 20 cents' worth of bottles each. Unfortunately we could not carry all the bottles and therefore had to hide some. Upon our return, however, some character had decided to bust the lot, leaving the fruits of our labour as just a pile of shattered glass.

Probably the funniest thing that happened during my childhood occurred in one of these half-constructed houses. Near one cracker night, we were playing chasings in a house that was being built at the end of our street. This was not an unusual way for us to pass time, but what made it memorable was the fact that we had some penny bungers to play with, and Eric, unable to wait to go to the toilet, decided to defecate on the ground inside the brickwork base of the house. The wooden floor work had not yet been completed and the house, at this stage, consisted of the brickwork base and the wooden frame.

Earlier that day we had amused ourselves by placing penny bungers in mud, lighting them and standing back to avoid the mud that was blasted all over the place by the exploding crackers. As a result, the freshly laid contents of Eric's bowels presented a great opportunity for further demolition work. With expert hands, Stephen, who, being older, knew the most about the strategic placing of explosives, inserted the two thunderbolts (which at 2 cents each were the most powerful crackers we could buy) into the brown, evil-smelling stool. As he prepared to ignite the crackers, the rest of us found 'safe' hiding spots. What followed was simply amazing.

Stephen lit the crackers and had only taken two steps towards safety when Mr Sharp, the cranky occupant of the house next door, put his head over the fence. 'What are you doing in there?' he boomed.

Startled by the voice, and forgetting about the rapidly approaching explosion, Stephen, who had his back to the fence, stopped and turned to locate the source of the voice. Rick, also taken by surprise, stood up from behind his cover and, as a reply formed on his lips, the explosion went off. The rest was pure bedlam.

Stephen took the brunt of the explosion, and as a result looked like he was wearing a camouflage outfit. You know, the type that has all those brown patches on it to break up a person's outline. Rick, who in standing up had placed himself between the source of the problem and Mr Sharp, also wore a fair amount of the flying debris. In standing there, however, Rick almost certainly saved Mr Sharp's face from a splattering. Those brown potions that could have hit Mr Sharp splattered against Rick's back. Others that missed Rick went hurtling past Mr Sharp to fall harmlessly in his yard. My brother and I, cleverly hidden behind a brick wall, escaped all consequences.

After the explosion no one moved for what seemed like hours, but what was in reality only a few seconds. Mr Sharp was flabbergasted, my brother and I remained hidden, and poor Steve could not believe what had happened to him. He just stood there, arms outstretched, looking at himself, his eyes opened wide in utter disbelief.

Marc recovered first. As the crackers were being lit he had

sought refuge by climbing the wooden frame. This was not the safest of hiding spots, as the mess on the lower part of his legs testified. After the initial shock of the explosion, he burst into loud, raucous laughter, quickly descended from his perch and took off. Rick, Eric, my brother and I followed suit. As looked back, our last sight of the house was Mr Sharp climbing the fence to grab Steve, who was still standing there, looking at himself in disbelief.

Perhaps Mr Sharp took pity on Steve, or maybe he managed to see the funny side of what had happened, but whatever the reason he let Steve go. Despite spending several anxious days waiting for Mr Sharp to contact our parents, nothing more came of it. Even at that young age, we realised that we owed Mr Sharp a very big favour.

A poem for Les Boyd

This poem has only had two performances. The first was for its intended recipient, Les Boyd; the second was when John Jansen read it out at Brian's funeral. It showed a side of him many people had not seen.

Brian wrote lots of silly poems over the years. I almost always got one in my birthday cards. His mother and many of his friends did too.

This is the only one I could find a copy of. I wish I had kept them all now.

The inaugural golf test match
By Banjo Johnson
'Brian, we're coming down to see you, we'll be there this weekend.'
On the phone spoke the voice of Les, my infamous friend.

'Great, we'll play golf when you get here,' was my keen reply,
'Make sure you bring your wallet 'cause the stakes they will be high.'

You could almost hear him thinking, 'How am I going to win?'
'Cause winning is important to this man who isn't thin.
'I know: I'll have to play him here, on my own home patch –
That'll give me the advantage in this Inaugural Golf Test Match.'

So excuses came thick and fast as to why down he could not come
'Perhaps you could come to Coota,' suggested my clever, scheming chum.
But to me, seeing friends was more important than the match.
Besides, I've seen Les play before – his golf isn't up to scratch.

So off we go to Coota to see our friends and have a hit,
Knowing of Les's home advantage, but caring not one bit.
On the first tee we stand, Les looking calm and cool,
He's thinking, 'So Brian actually came to Coota – I'll thrash that naive fool!'

He even brought Daryl and the Arab to see his win
So confident was this man who isn't thin.
Up the first we headed, to start this great contest
Les wearing only short sleeves, Brian in sloppy joe and vest.

The first few holes were even, no one hit the front.
I was just unlucky, while Les played like a c—.
Then with daring play and enterprise, I built a two-stroke lead,
Les was very worried 'cause winning is his need.

But a mongrel 12 on just one hole tore this lead apart,
Fortunately for me, however, I've got a monstrous heart.
To beat Les now, I knew, would require better things from me,
So I bravely tapped in for a par, then got another three.

Yes four quick pars in a row, and Les's winning plan is shattered,
But once I came up here to see my mate, to me winning never mattered.
So I play a few holes poorly to keep him in the hunt,
I try to give him a little hope, but he still plays like a c—.

And soon the match is over, and Les is feeling blue
'Cause Les finished with 112, I got 102.
So, Les, the moral of this story is that whatever schemes you plan,
You need more than home advantage to beat a better man.

www.ingramcontent.com/pod-product-compliance
Lightning Source LLC
Chambersburg PA
CBHW062033290426
44109CB00026B/2611